To Ken
Enjoy the read.

GAMES PIMPS PLAY:
PIMPS, PLAYERS AND WIVES-IN-LAW

A Quantitative Analysis
of Street Prostitution

James F. Hodgson

Foreword by
Livy Visano

D0841398

Canadian Scholars' Press   Toronto   1997

Games Pimps Play: Pimps, Players and Wives-In-Law
A Quantitative Analysis of Street Prostitution
James F. Hodgson

First published in 1997 by
Canadian Scholars' Press Inc.
180 Bloor Street West, Ste. 402
Toronto, Ontario
M5S 2V6

Canadian Cataloguing in Publication Data

Hodgson, James Fredrick, 1958–
    Games pimps play : pimps, players and wives-in-law : a quantitative analysis of street prostitution

Includes bibliographical references.
ISBN 1-55130-116-4

1. Prostitution. 2. Pimps. 3. Prostitutes. I. Title.

HQ117.H62 1997   306.74'2   C96-932302-6

Page layout and cover design by Brad Horning

This book explores the world of pimping
and identifies the "games pimps play"
with the lives of women and children.

Acknowledgements

This research project began in 1983 as part of an honours thesis effort and has evolved into a sociological journey of many years. The years of research, writing, observing, interviewing and rewriting have provided me with a perspective of street life that continues to influence my life today. I am forever indebted to the young people who showed great courage and determination in sharing their experiences with an outsider. The honest and forthright details that these young people disclosed allowed this exploratory study to depict street life as illustrated by people who were living it. I thank these many young people for their honesty, trust and determination in sharing their lives to explicate and add creditability to this research project. I have learned much from their perseverance, diligence and resolve.

Multiple drafts of this exploratory study have been read and edited over the years by a number of talented and exceptional people, including Evelyn Hansen, Angela Bell-Irving, Kathy Orban, Beverly McKeddie and Camilla Mahan. I am forever indebted to these people for their time and patience in providing research and literary assistance.

My colleague, friend and mentor Dr. Livy A. Visano has been an essential source in providing the appropriate academic guidance and development. Dr. Visano has provided much inspiration and has been the derivation of encouragement in the completion of this exploratory study. His commitment to educational and intellectual pursuits provides for a model that many wish to emulate. I am eternally grateful for his commitment and patience in walking me along the pathway to academic enlightenment.

To my family, who I owe much in the form of gratitude and appreciation. I thank my father, William Thomas Hodgson, for his continual display of unconditional love, tolerance and support during the term of this research exercise. His much earlier lesson of "never give up" has been most useful during this project. Most of all, I thank my best friend and partner Camilla Anne Mahan for her unrelenting support, companionship and determination. Her commitment to me and this project has facilitated the closure of this undertaking. Her lesson of "living your dreams" has brought many years of research to a conclusion. To these two very extraordinary people in my life I dedicate this book.

James F. Hodgson
1997

Contents

List of Tables

From Localized Texts to Hegemonic Narratives: Contextualizing the "Games People Play"

Review and Overview: Setting the Stage

Games Pimps Play is a rich, original and compellingly comprehensive study of various stages of development and transformation of vice, violence and victimization. The general argument of this book is advanced within a set of deceptively simplistic, consistently cogent and well-substantiated claims. This book offers new and provocative insights into prostitution and the concomitant enterprises of pimping by translating street life as a complex configuration of occupational values and subterranean economies. Professor Hodgson's analysis takes great pains to challenge the reductionist, facile and obfuscating conceptions of street prostitution, so characteristic of conventional approaches, by reiterating the more dynamic, elusive and complex interactions of contexts, activities and actors within specified socio-political sites. Professor Hodgson demonstrates that prostitution, as a concept, is not necessarily a single cohesive abstraction with normative, consensual or static orientations. Rather, prostitution is an expression of both defiance and deference to rules; prostitution is a consequence of both conflict and consensus; and, prostitution exists within contexts of gendered subjectivities and multiple constitutions. Within the socio-cultural narratives of prostitution, Professor Hodgson succeeds in demonstrating that identity is a construction of cultural, political and social forms that intersect talk and text. This perspective is intellectually promising. In other words, this theme provides refreshingly candid and engagingly fertile insights into the competing and converging discourses that implicate wider texts of exclusion—notably power relations, the fetish of materialism and individualism. These respective themes encourage an appreciation of both the conditions and consequences of marginalizing the "other." To elucidate, the designation of "prostitute" evokes images not of pleasure but of pain. Accordingly, the prostitute is a commodity, the value of which is determined by others, notably the pimp, the police, moral entrepreneurs, etc.

For Professor Hodgson, the devaluation of the prostitute as an item of exchange is part of a discourse that justifies control. *Games Pimps Play* challenges the socially constructed and historically rooted social orders by interrogating sources of contradiction, profit and power. The book articulates the nature of cultural controls and contesting contexts. Clearly, this book critically examines diverse interpretive schemes (cultural codes), accounts or excuses (linguistic devices) and neutralization techniques (survival strategies) of all actors implicated in the world of prostitution. In fact, culture as a calculus frames experience, supplies interpretations from which inferences are drawn, legitimates decisions, provides a history and secures a loyalty to rules. Unlike traditional accounts, which tend to stress the essentialism of binary codes based on artificial assumptions of a banal morality, this book presents prostitution and pimping as interrelated, blurred and overlapping phenomena.

The literature on prostitution, from empirical inquiries to more popular novels, pays considerable attention to the views of street prostitutes. Interestingly, the other side of this cash-for-sex nexus, the pimp, is simply depicted as a mass of undifferentiated identities. Indeed, research on prostitution has not scrutinized, let alone analyzed, pimp-prostitute relations (Benjamin, 1985; Dixon, 1989; Visano, 1987; 1990; 1991). Professor Hodgson's discussion of how pimps organize their activities and deploy their resources in order to secure control is a formidable contribution to the field of criminology.

Specifically, procurement, as a form of seduction or abduction, is shaped by various stages of "getting started," "fitting in," "applying the trade" as well as contingencies (self concept, reactions of others, the skills of the operator). This career taxonomy is analyzed in terms of aspirations and frustrations, anxieties that include failed expectations in the normative order, the discoveries of escape and the tyranny of violence. Pushed from a number of abusive circumstances that predate the street scene and pulled towards the excitement of "Saturday night," drugs, shelter, the glitter of the "fast lane," a seemingly comforting network of associates, lucrative rewards, etc. Pimps succeed in creating images that facilitate the construction of a false consciousness in the minds of "their" workers. Security is the price of coercion within the craft of pimping. More significantly, this focus calls into question issues of authority and status "on the street." In operationalizing their conception of change as struggles, prostitutes signal the importance of ideology in framing their respective levels of accommodation and resistance. That is, survival strategies politicize a morality of consensus and conflict (seduction and abduction). The author considers the much overlooked dimensions of seduction as a moment of cooperation within conflictive contexts. By analyzing the significance of needs and emerging vested interests, Professor Hodgson recognizes that what is at stake is power, resources that shape the life-chances of marginalized women. Power is the ability to disarticulate and misappropriate the experiences of others. The bodies of these dependents are vulgarized as instant money machines. These transformed bodies and manipulated minds are animated according to the disciplinary cadence of their pimps' voices. Young street kids are especially vulnerable to the games played by seasoned hustlers (Sheehy,1971; Visano, 1987; Weisberg, 1985). A number of multilayered problems characterize "life on the street," ranging from the poverty of hunger, homelessness, under- or unemployment and illiteracy, to deep emotional and psychological scars. As Professor Hodgson reiterates, the "helping" hand disguises the machinations of social control, a mode of containment that maintains the status of the periphery. Pacified as docile learners and infantilized as "fresh" commodities, the economically destitute are served benevolent palliatives, which sedate the more troublesome consequences of marginality (Jackson, 1981). For instance, pimps feel compelled to manage the routine lives of "their" prostitutes, to maintain their investments with a minimum of cost. Violence remains a ubiquitous backdrop in the reproduction of a street order that privileges the pimp.

Cultural enslavement is a condition of social freedom. Social beings are constituted in the context of cultural control. As a text, the street culture is an expression of ideologies based on survival. Awareness is culturally mediated and linguistically conditioned. How can prostitutes be expected to deconstruct codes of thinking and critically elaborate on the conditions and consequences of their own oppression?

The book breaks new ground by focussing on the processual and structural dimensions of prostitution by confronting directly the conditions and consequences of abuse. This book knits together existing and new knowledge about the social organization of violence, thereby contributing to future research designs that would be pursued by scholars studying relations of ruling.

Culture figures prominently in the survival strategies. For Professor Hodgson, prostitution is a text that must not only be contextualized within the political economy of pimping but also within the wider hegemony of mainstream cultural values. Gender and class inequalities prevalent in the dominant culture permeate social relations on the street (Carman and Moody, 1985). The interplay of multiple misfortunes continues to subject women on the street to the periphery. Herein lies the conceptual problematic: the routine lives of prostitutes are deeply ensconced in constraining cultural exigencies of survival. Professor Hodgson questions their shallow rhetorical claims of emancipation and the street values that celebrate non conformity. Moreover, *Games Pimps Play* delves into issues that to date have been too glibly dismissed or overlooked in extant studies of prostitutes and pimps. For instance, how do prostitutes legitimate the exceedingly intrusive role played by their pimps? In turn, how accommodating are pimp-prostitute relations? What about the risks of resistance? As the author admonishes, a prudent investigation can ill afford to ignore actors and their various subjectivities.

This study of pimps clarifies a number of generic processes to which a large number of communities continue to be exposed. This book succeeds in providing a valuable touchstone for further theorizing and should be read not only by social scientists but by anyone interested in appreciating the dialectics of conflict, development and transformation. This work is a solid contribution to the sociologies of inequality, moral regulation, social change and social control. It is undoubtedly suitable for many audiences, from those more oriented toward multidisciplinary accounts, cultural studies, sociology of communities, gender and sex to the more curious general public readers.

The discussion of the relationship between the sex trade workers and state authorities is also very persuasive and in a number of instances sheds new light on the interactions between politics and "colonized" communities of workers. The author has used this focus skilfully and profitably in juxtaposing conscience and convenience of interventive strategies. For example, the contradictions between the raging "war on drugs" and the "benevolence " of armies of crusaders divert attention from the fundamental etiological concerns thereby exacerbating effective local initiatives that empower sex trade workers (Lowman, 1984). This theme of prevailing contradictions deserves careful scrutiny because it is so clearly and passionately developed and because it is based on a well-researched literature review. Unlike the more traditional ethnographic street studies, which fail to implicate the state, Hodgson interprets state enterprises as manipulations, negotiations and political contests. This study, therefore, stimulates a number of challenging questions about state agents, which subsequent researchers are encouraged to investigate. This endeavour serves as an excellent application of the current debates in sociology with regard to the role of the state in shaping consciousness and subjectivity; the links between micro- and macro-sociological inquiries; and the carceral connections of political economy and its attendant seductive ideological appeals. This convenient obsession with danger, risks, the ideology of law and order transforms the common prostitute into a criminal, rather than a complainant, witness or victim. The marginalization of gender, race, age and class facilitates this punitive focus. This book is catalytic in its ability to transform readers into active observers and to encourage them to unravel the promises and paradoxes of the sex trade. For example, within the contexts of social control, readers are encouraged to assess the appropriateness of police "crackdowns" and undercover operations.

The phenomenon of policing prostitution cannot be appreciated without a fundamental knowledge of that which informs extant police strategies. Evidently, the latter are restricted to reactive law enforcement roles rather than crime prevention, order maintenance or social services, especially police tasks. Also, policing tends to be confined to public spaces. The institutions of law and privacy inhibit the regulation of moral offences. As a result of occasional complaints—usually from merchants, politicians or resident associations, the police respond more aggressively. Typically, police authorities reduce prostitution to a juridic and analgesic chatter of crime and its risk. Increasingly, the police have relied on prostitutes as fertile sources of information. Police officers seek to develop legal lines of credit with prostitutes. That is, effective investigations by intelligence, morality or even uniformed officers require the development of a network of street informants. In return for disclosing information to the police, street prostitutes hope for a promise of leniency in their own legal circumstances. It is clear that legal authorities exploit the vulnerability of street hustlers (Visano, 1990b). Like the procurers, the police prey on the susceptibilities of newcomers.

Professor Hodgson highlights the significance of illusions and credulities in generating occupational models. The empirical analyses of the local occupational cultures serve to balance work and play. By resorting to a talk of a "game," pimps refuse to acknowledge the pain they inflict on prostitutes. The "games" pimps play acquire meanings in terms of the signs and signifiers and rules and roles. In time, the game becomes naturalized as prevailing common sense or "street smarts." Pimps appeal to a particular loyalty to the "game," a game with risks and rewards. Seasoned "players" develop a rights-based discourse that enables them to transform prostitutes into winners and/ or losers. Even as a metaphor, the notion of a game is based on a relational view of street life. The component elements of this social order are not individuals or institutions but combinations of vulnerabilities like age, class, gender, race, and criminal records, etc. that constitute social relations. Even though prostitution emphasizes fleeting, emotionally detached and mercenary exchanges, the contexts of the "workplace as a game" condition work attitudes and activities.

The game imagery is attractive to newcomers, the majority of whom are youths. Pimps glorify the game and play into its existentialist "presentism" (Cusson, 1983) of youth. A youth-oriented culture pervades all street relations. Myths flourish about the significance of age, which becomes a cultural marker that degrades older prostitutes as pathetic sexual actors (McPhersen, 1983). Images of the game are consistent with images of youth. Both stereotypes characterize the world of pimping. The game imagery ensures both dependency and detachment; it is only a game, the rules of which are set by the pimp. And youthfulness secures greater marketability and profit for the pimp given the premium placed on youthful bodies (Harris, 1973; Lloyd, 1977). Clients prize youthfulness (Fontana, 1984; Linedecker, 1981). Interestingly, this book asks: To what extent do the "games" played by pimps maintain the collective conscience of street communities, that is, a binding moral consensus?

Readers are asked to situate themselves in the debates and struggles that characterize the study of pimps, to ground their perceptions, to avoid closures, to empower themselves conceptually and to engage in open dialogue. This book challenges the congested closures of criminological canons by defying the defining gaze of legal and illegitimate authorities. Traditional texts obscure power relations. Confining discussions of prostitution to a litany of legal criteria is a meaningless exercise that forecloses the possibility of engaging in social justice discourses. As Habermas (1974) indicated, the meanings and symbols of the dominant ideology prevent critical thinking by penetrating social processes, language and individual consciousness.

The dominant order scripts prostitution as an instance of pathology. Again, this book succeeds in demonstrating that pimping and prostitution are not just incidental elements of our social order; the violence attendant with these insidiously exploitative projects go to the very core of political, cultural and economic conditions. Hegemony is central to an analysis of identity and cultural practices and how differences emerge as responses to domination, as people live out the subject positions available to them. At a more generic level, prostitution is a metaphor that transforms history into nature. The aim of metaphors as linguistic devices is to depict as natural the performative aspects while concealing the more coercive aspects of this enterprise such as pimping. Pimping as an authority system signifies form, identity and cultural practices. Differences emerge as responses to domination at the everyday level, which is predatory (McLaren, 1995).

This original investigation examines the attitudes and activities—the subjectivities of local actors and reactors. This study on hustler-client relations incorporates a multimethod design of informal interviews, observations of streetcorner transactions and structured diaries. Professor Hodgson adopts a flexible "theoretical sampling" scheme (Glaser and Strauss, 1967) that is well-suited and convenient, which generates leads to well-informed contacts. Independent introductions are also made by going directly to the natural setting. Methodologically, the author's judicious use of a variety of data collection strategies is laudable. This "triangulated" approach elicites a wealth of evidence from interview materials, a plethora of government documents, on-site observations, consultations and statistics from public and private sources. In the course of his visits and re-visits to the setting, he presents both cross-sectional and longitudinal data, which are incorporated very successfully in the analysis. Additionally, the author's circumspect life histories are particularly impressive in the careful mapping of complex institutional configurations.

An ethnography essentially encourages the researcher to grasp a first-hand knowledge about the social world in question, to experience the actors' experiences in their "everyday worlds." As a general methodology, an ethnography displays an "omnibus quality" by incorporating an array of well-reasoned exercises that include informal observations, direct observation and participation, conversational or informal interviewing and formal, unfocused interviews, as well as more egocentric inquiries, reflexivity and self-debates. Flexibility invites researchers to be more responsive to changing situations and more open to pursuing issues and leads in greater detail. An immersion in the everyday life of actors reflects a respect of "appreciation." Only by getting close to these "hosts" (Wax, 1980:272) and spending time on their "turf" can the investigator discover the social construction of action. An appreciative stance demands a superior standard of sensitivity and an immediate willingness to explore matters that are meaningful to others. Experience is the beginning moment of a method of an analysis that does not lose sight of its location in actual lived realities (Smith, 1988, 1990).

An ethnography is extremely appropriate in researching that which remains hidden from official content analyses, notably the lives of populations designated as criminal. People in their natural "turf" tend to share information more readily with those who participate in their life or with others who indicate a more sensitive appreciation of their setting and activities. Ethnographies usually commence with only a few general concepts or "hunches" regarding the nature of social organizations. Under the general guidance of orienting concepts, data are collected on how actors organize their worlds, "make sense of their social order." Gradually, the investigator organizes the data by sorting out similar and different contents into tentative formulations of categories. A number of constructs emerge as a result of these theoretical interpretations of empirical incidents. An ethnography facilitates the development of a moral insight.

An ethnography makes effective use of the relationships that researchers establish with their studied populations (subjects) in the field. The rapport and subsequent information collected are conditioned by the context in which researchers are placed; relations are typically constructed within processes of reciprocity. To ensure a naturalistic description, a role is required that is comfortable enough for the studied populations (subjects) to accept and comfortable enough for the researcher to assume. This role includes movements back and forth, between the world of one's hosts and one's own sociological discipline. Responsibility requires abilities to respond to authentic voices by furnishing researchers with occasions that enable them to be aware of the external world that corresponds with their ideas. Human beings are at the centre of their experiences, subjects in their world.

Authenticity encourages an analytic awareness of the other by avoiding elements of social paralysis. There is a connection to be made between the self as subject and the other by deconstructing the location of the self in society. Consequently, authenticity considers the self as a knowing being, a powerful self that possesses a clear understanding of one's place or "habitus" in the world. The social construction of the subjectivity process implicates the production of identity by highlighting the discursive narratives of selfhood.

Behind the Game and beyond Pimping: Moving Forward from Local to Global Contests

Culture is a constructed text that is historically rooted in male privilege. Cultural codes frame modes of thinking—beliefs and ideas that in turn govern human conduct. Moreover, social institutions like prostitution structure core values of dominant ideologies that promote the unique location of women in society. In both direct and more subtle ways, the dominant or master culture conceals and reveals practices that silence, differentiate and condition subordination. Culture reinforces the exclusion of women from full and meaningful participation in social life. In brief, inequality is inscribed in the dominant culture that has traditionally deviantized and subsequently incarcerated women. The tragic imperative of this cultural conditioning is the social control of women, the reproduction of hegemonic conceptual schemes that facilitate the legitimation of oppression. The devaluation of women, for example, belongs to meta discourses (cultural givens) that inferiorize, alienate and violate women in all aspects of their personal and social lives. It is, therefore, impossible for women to find themselves in the existing culture. Instead, women encounter themselves as echoes (Rowbotham, 1989:287).

Clearly, from aggressive sexual consumerism (Clark and Lewis, 1977), the economic dependence of women (Dobash and Dobash, 1979) and the oppressive ideology of the family (Freeman, 1982) to the eroticization of violence (MacKinnon, 1982)—to name only a few cultural projects—males as a group constitute the dominant class while females are unequivocally dismissed as a deviant class. In North American society the concept of a male is normalized while that of a female is marginalized and deviantized. As Schur argues, "to be female is to be deviant by definition in the prevailing culture" (1980:23). Given that the male culture has been consistently promoted and protected, women have asked: "Where is our history? What is our culture?... Have we contributed nothing to our human heritage?....It is very difficult to discover ourselves in the existing culture" (Leavitt, 1976:1).

Sexism, or more appropriately misogyny, characterizes privileged cultural positions. History incorporates women only if their experiences are subsumed under male norms and values. Women have been and continue to be removed from ideological and cultural reproductions. The feminist struggle against the patriarchal control of women (Currie and Kline, 1991) requires ongoing confrontations on many sites, both conceptually and substantively.

In this discussion we move beyond traditional androcentric models that have far too frequently distorted women's experiences. The illusory nature of patriarchal orthodoxies or, as Cott (1987) notes, the perpetuation of gendered hierarchies in everyday life, is challenged. The world of pimping advances only male knowledge and understanding. In general this ideological practice problematizes the many challenges posed by feminist scholars. Within all traditional male-controlled worksites, the power to create the world from one's limited vantage point is power in its male form (MacKinnon, 1982). Power is essentially a form of masculinity (MacKinnon, 1987:53). The struggles of women resisting male-dominated assumptions are seldom acknowledged. Prostitution is reflective of this one-sided, male standpoint. In essence, pimping invites conceptual imperialism; images of women are always mediated through men's eyes. Prostitution has been, so far, constructed by some men for the benefit of men. The dominant ideology maintains this patriarchy. Studies like *Games Pimps Play* indicate that no longer can the experiences of women be overlooked as inconsequential or even marginal. It is essential to look into the "lived-in" experiences of women. The primacy of the lived experiences of women must be incorporated as a central agenda in re-framing and grounding underlying assumptions about social control.

As previously noted, the exploitation of women is ubiquitous—from the coverage of fashion, food, human interest stories in daily newspapers and the advertisements in women's magazines to prime-time and day-time soap operas. Collectively, the coverage of women in the print and electronic media strives to create a docility wherein women's needs are defined according to socializing or acculturating consumerism that defines consumption as a basic need (Ollman, 1976:75-88). This obsession with the woman's body prevails as long as the woman remains male property. As Farrell (1989:16) cogently notes:

> Materialism functions as a rage and a shield...we are subject to its ideology and dogma as a part of modern social life. It sticks, endures, and multiplies as social redundancy...we are made slave to its functionality and form. To be part of social life we are required to speak through it as it captures and confines the way we interrelate with one another.

The body is docile whenever it is subjected, used, transformed and improved (Foucault,1977:136, 1980). Women's bodies are commercialized in order to attract consumers to certain products. Influenced by corporate profits, the body "sexualizes" a product that otherwise would go unnoticed. This body, in turn, is appropriated and distorted by the product. Women have long been manipulated and held hostage to such hegemonic cultural stereotypes sustained by the fashion industry, an enterprise animated only by its incredible profits. Women's bodies have always been considered a "sight to be seen" (Berger, 1988). The popular culture has transformed the woman's body according to a plethora of commodity fetishes. The body has been rendered incomplete and unattractive unless disciplined and designed by fashionable images of beauty.

Traditional gender socialization shapes all aspects of everyday life. Degrading rituals persist from the more public behaviour in institutions of work, education, leisure and sports to the more private domains of family dynamics, dating behaviour and sexual practices. Dominant socialization processes attribute roles to women that emphasize the significance of reproduction and motherhood as well as the attendant qualities of nurturing, care and passivity (Mackie, 1987; Lips, 1991). As an instrument of social control, socialization perpetuates the status quo—traditions replete with distortions and mythologies about women's bodies.

Prior to capitalism, a patriarchal system was well established in which men controlled the labour of women, especially in the household. In fact, as Hartmann (1979:230) maintains, capitalism grew on top of patriarchy; therefore, patriarchal capitalism is a stratified society par excellence. The emergence of capitalism required social control over the labour power of women. Patriarchy shaped the form of modern capitalism just as capitalism transformed patriarchal institutions (Hartmann, 1979:208). Capitalism served to bifurcate more clearly the production of goods and services into the public and private spheres. In the public domain the production of goods and impersonal services in organizations was characterized by wage labour and the development of surplus. Private production involved personal goods and services in the context of the household. Unpaid household labour and the surplus of work occurred to satisfy the needs of those members who do not contribute—men. Public and private exploitation of labour are interrelated. The interaction between capitalism and patriarchy shaped the status of women in all labour market transactions (Hartmann, 1979:230).

Capitalism extended men's control over the labour power of women in both the public (wage labour system) and the private (household chores) spheres. Class domination is a fundamental feature of capitalism. But, it is a social order in which the dominant class is composed mainly of men. In this context it is as capitalists that men derive their power (McIntosh, 1978:259). As a dominant economic order, capitalism relies heavily on differences—divisions in labour, inequalities in wages and conflicts among labourers—that facilitate further exploitation. The impetuses are accumulation—profits and investments achieved by eliminating competition and stimulating demand.

Job segregation is a fundamental instrument in maintaining male superiority. Consequently, women were kept dependent on men and ensured the differential allocation of resources. The existence of the family and the dependency of women upon their husband's wages (Beechey, 1978:187) served to break down male workers' resistance. Capitalism used women as unskilled, underpaid labour to undercut male workers (Hartmann, 1979:230). Simply, Marx's theory of value provides an understanding of both exchange value and use value. Crudely, a product has these two values: the *use value* is defined according to the value of the product in satisfying needs; the *exchange value* is related to its transformation into a commodity related to other products and thereby exchanged (Israel, 1971:41-45). In capitalism, workers produce a surplus to be exchanged. Thus, workers and their labour power acquire exchange value and a commodity status. The worker's labour power is transformed into a commodity readily bought and sold. Wage is an exchange value. The case of domestic labour however is significantly different.

Domestic labour exists outside of the marketplace but is nevertheless crucial to capitalism for it is responsible for the reproduction of labour power. Women's labour provides the physical and psychological maintenance necessary for the reproduction of labour power (Luxton, 1978:35). Domestic labour, therefore, has a use- alue. The woman therein is a service station attendant for capitalist enterprises (Smith, 1973). Production and reproduction, the economic base of society, dialectically influence and are influenced by the superstructure. As Harris (1981:63) elaborates: "Under capitalism, the separation of domestic labour from socialized production coincides with the distinction between the production of use values and the production of exchange values in the forms of commodities." The need for wage labour in capitalism is congruent with the patriarchal needs for the institution of motherhood (Eisenstein, 1983; Currie, 1986; Currie and Klein, 1991:13). Female wage labour is devalued since women are assumed to be subsidiary workers. These dual roles of domestic and wage labour result in the creation of an industrial reserve army.

In addition, violence against women is a coercive form of social control that expresses male dominance. To be a woman is to experience terror at the hands of men (Stanko, 1985:9; Beirne and Messerschmidt, 1991:520). All aspects of male intimidation—physical, emotional and psychological—seek to maintain masculine privilege, that is, male supremacy. However, this power to victimize and subordinate women is socially structured. Clearly, the juxtaposition of a patriarchal culture and capitalism grossly enhances the vulnerability of women in everyday life. As Smart (1981:57) notes, it is essential to examine precisely how social, economic and political orders are so reliant upon a power inequality between the sexes. Intrinsic to such an investigation is an analysis of the way in which the State operates to reproduce power inequality, that is an enquiry into the role of law in that reproduction (Smart, 1981). Institutions, therefore, like the family, law and politics, reproduce the tyranny of violence against women. In fact, systemic wars have been waged against women (French, 1992:19). As French explains, only feminist analysts treat male violence towards women as a global crisis. By simply treating violence towards women as individual acts, journalists, social scientists and social workers trivialize the underlying politics of the real situation (French, 1992:22). Traditional approaches "white wash" men, and in the process preclude intelligent public discussion.

Specifically, law and its agencies of the criminal justice system act in ways that reinforce a woman's place in male society (Chesney-Lind, 1992:165). Only feminist perspectives are sensitive to the experiences of women. Feminist approaches have long demonstrated that girls are more frequently the recipients of violence and sexual abuse; gender and sexual scripts found in patriarchal families facilitate the violence against women; girls who run away from this abuse are forced to become escaped convicts taking to the streets for survival; and girls get involved in crimes that exploit their sexual object status (Chesney-Lind, 1992:67).

Women are perceived by agents of the criminal justice system to be weaker and in need of protection (Visher, 1983). For decades the criminal justice system was guided by notions of chivalry. Chivalry refers to men's unwillingness to inflict harm on a woman, combined with a disbelief that a woman could be a real offender (Pollack, 1961; Crew, 1991:60). Likewise, this paternalism in law adopted the attitude that women are childlike and therefore in need of protection. Accordingly, women are not responsible for their actions (Crew, 1991:60). An emphasis on chivalry/paternalism results in more leniency. Familial paternalism—having dependants—is a criterion for leniency and reform (Erez, 1989:309). So-called "fallen" women like prostitutes are perceived to be in need of guidance and protection (Smart, 1976). This imagery of the fallen or hardened woman has historically invited harsh penalties because she has repudiated fundamental social values. To repeat, girls are more harshly penalized for any behaviour deemed undesirable or inappropriate, while boys are almost expected or even condoned to be delinquent because they are more readily seen to be going through an adolescent "phase" (Chesney-Lind and Sheldon, 1992). Different criteria are used when arresting women (Visher, 1983:22), such as demeanour, marital status, moral standing, etc . In the contemporary North American culture, the legal treatment of women is anchored in gendered expectations. In the study of prostitution, social order is not only a gendered but also a racialized reality.

Racism is integrally related to the process of designating deviance. In fact, racism is a resource for formulating and formatting practices of exclusion. This mechanism of racism constructs and commoditizes deviant discourses. The phenomenon of racism differentiates, marginalizes and negates identity. In North America, blacks live within two concentric circles of segregation. One imprisons them because of colour while the other confines them within a separate culture of poverty (King, 1964:23).There is an overrepresentation of blacks as offenders in the criminal justice system and a corresponding underrepresentation of blacks in positions of authority. In Mississippi in the past five years, forty-eight grisly jail cell deaths (over one-half of them blacks) have been ruled as suicides (NAACP,1993: 24). Disturbingly, twenty-four percent of all black men in their twenties are in jail, prison or on parole; one in ten Hispanic men; one in sixteen white men in the USA. In other words, 1,054,508 white men are in same category, representing 6.2 percent of the 20-29 age group. Racial disparities for women are also overwhelmingly disproportionate. In fact, 1 per 100 white women is involved in criminal justice system compared to 37 per 100 for black women (*Boston Globe*, 3,03,1990). Again, one out of every two African American men is likely to be arrested during his lifetime; one out of four black men between the ages of 20 and 29 is incarcerated, on probation or on parole. A black man is 7.5 times more likely to be arrested than a white man. Black men constitute six percent of the general population in the USA and yet represent forty-four percent of the prison inmates. Racial inequality pervades society and is reflected in the justice system and reproduced in prisons (Weinstein and Cummins, 1993:41). This percentage of blacks far exceeds their representation in the population. By 1993 in the United States, African Americans suffered incarceration rates of over 3,000 per 100,000—six times the national average. A focus on the "ideology of hopelessness" (Massey and Denton, 1993:5) that accompanies poverty must implicate an analysis of the economic, political and social structures that perpetuate inequalities—racism. It costs 2.5 billion dollars annually to monitor and punish black males (*Washington Post*, 27,02,1990: A3).

The media and policing authorities have perpetuated stereotypes about the incidence of "black crime," ethnic crime and crimes committed by refugees and illegal immigrants. Network news in the United States does not report on black Americans. It reports most often on a stereotype called "the black" or "the Negro" (Effron, 1971:144). The media typically attribute increased crime rates to an unruly black underclass (Cashmore and McLaughlin, 1991:3).

Racism is a coherent expression of hegemonic imperatives. Silence, therefore, ensures its survival; struggle and the repositioning of identities are essential, especially for whites who have long enjoyed the benefits of racism and colonialism. A strident movement, not token gestures of state sponsored multiculturalism, is required strategically. Political movements are the result of years of struggle. As Malcolm X wrote:

> Well, I believe it's a crime for anyone who is brutalized to continue to accept that brutality without doing something to defend himself...I don't speak against the sincere well-meaning, good white people. I have learned that there are some. I have learned that not all white people are racists. I am speaking against and my fight is against white racists. I firmly believe that Negroes have the right to fight against these racists, by any means that are necessary
>
> *1970:366-367*

As former Black Panther Party leader Dhoruba Bin Wahad stated: "Racism is not a problem black people have. It's a problem that white people have" (Lines, 1992a:26). Likewise, as Lines reported, activists Stokely Carmichael and Charles Hamilton argued:

> One of the most disturbing things about almost all white supporters has been that they are reluctant to go into their own communities—which is where racism exists—and work to get rid of it....It is hoped that eventually there will be a coalition of poor blacks and poor whites... creating a poor-white block dedicated to the goals of a free, open society—not one based on racism and subordination.... The main responsibility of this task falls upon whites.... Only whites can mobilize and organize those communities along the lines necessary and possible for effective alliances with black communities...political modernization process must involve the white community as well as the black.
>
> *(Carmichael and Hamilton, 1967:81-83)*

Racism needs to be defined in terms of power and understood as it positions whites in the centre of dominant discourses, occupying positions of authority and power while others are relegated to places of marginality and inferiority (Hall, 1981: 9, 17). Racism is an ideology propagated by institutions of the dominant culture. Racist ideas are internalized and expressed as truths. Racist images find expression in state practices and policies. In the world of prostitution prevailing racist stereotypes emerge about the terror of black pimps. Colour and criminality have become synonymous. A number of questions are seldom raised. Why is there an overrepresentation on a per capita basis of colour and street prostitution? How is colour represented in suite crimes? How are racist stereotypes used to justify police interventions? How is colour vertically stratified in the world of organized crime and prostitution? What is the role of drugs in the world of pimping? How is the current "war on drugs" (the focus on the supply side) designed to exacerbate the evils of pimping? What core values in North American society promote prostitution and pimping?

Lastly, the culture of capital, filtered through an ideology of liberalism, rewards power and privileges the ethos of possessive individualism. The prevailing materialist culture destroys the dignity of those individuals, organizations and communities designated as "others." Moreover, moral regulation is constructed within a framework of sophisticated surveillance, characteristic of industrial and post-industrial societies. This ubiquitous regulation is legitmated by institutions that promote a particular peace that protects cherished ideals of privacy and property. Typically in our society, privacy and property are articulated within a well-respected utilitarian framework of liberalism. Indeed, individualism and materialism have become interchangeable in opposing access to equality of opportunities and condition. Moreover, the dominant culture, supported by agencies of control, rewards the privileged while pathologizing the poor. Not only do we marginalize the poor but as a society we condemn them to a life of misery, to a life that is constantly at risk—far more susceptible to physical, emotional and mental illnesses, the dangers of survival, shorter life expectancies, more stressful family relationships, guaranteed illiteracy, etc.

The texts of prostitution and pimping are contextually determined and discursively shaped according to narratives of inequality that include misogyny, racism and capitalism. The texts of prostitution and pimping within the context of a prevailing materialism that defines dignity by dollars negates humanity. Prostitution and pimping are not confined to the street but are routine features in relations of ruling. Like many exclusionary projects, prostitution and pimping deprive actors of the means "to participate in creating forms of thought relevant or adequate to express their own experience or to define and raise consciousness about their situation and concerns" (Smith, 1987: 18). According to Smith (1990: 210-211), textual mediated forms of social organization involve the dependence upon and exploitation of the textual capacity to crystallize and preserve inequalities. The power of the pimp rests in the authority of the text. The text of prostitution mediates narratives of inequalities. Although more vulgar and visible, the games played by pimps follow the script that has been traditionally cherished and continually celebrated: possessive individualism. Irrespective of its different guise—"taking the edge," "the hustle," "survival of the fittest," "doing business," "survival of the slickest," etc., the game is both a product of values imported from the dominant order as well as a reflection of subcultural street values that have evolved as a folk wisdom of "street smarts" oriented towards survival. Prostitution is complicated, defying banal explanations. The law, however, tends to seek to avoid this truth by creating distractions and by offering simple remedies. As Patricia Williams (1991:10-11) advises, "challenging, playing with these as rhetorical gestures is, it seems to me, necessary for any conception of justice." Lastly, Luce Irigaray (1985:84-85) suggests that:

women are "products" used and exchanged by men. Their status is that of merchandise, "commodities".... Commodities ...do not take themselves to market on their own.... What would become...if women, who have been only objects of consumption or exchange...were to become "speaking subjects" as well.

In conclusion, *Games Pimps Play* invites readers to challenge dominant cultural discourses and to reconstruct a more critical interrogation of power. Informed by progressive social justice orientations, this book highlights theoretically the foundations of the wider culture, especially the centrality of coercion. With reference to prostitution, this book argues that the study of meanings is inseparable from the study of culture. In this regard, Lyotard (1984:15) admonishes:

A self does not amount to much, but no self is an island; each exists in the fabric of relations that is now more complex and mobile than ever before. Young or old, man or woman, rich or poor, a person is always located at "nodal points" or specific communication circuits, however tiny these may be. Or better: one is always located at a post through which various kinds of messages pass.

In brief, both the positions of prostitute and pimp are constructed in contradictions as acting subjects and subjected actors.

L. A. Visano
Chair, Department of Sociology
Atkinson College
York University

References

Beechey, V. "Women and Production: A Critical Analysis of Some Sociological Theories of Women's Work." In A. Kuhn and A.M. Wolp, eds. *Feminism and Materialism: Women and Modes of Production* London: Routledge and Kegan Paul, 1978.

Beirne, P. and J. Messerschmidt. *Criminology*. New York: Harcourt, Brace and Jovanovich, 1991.

Benjamin, M. *Juvenile Prostitution: A Portrait of the Life*. Toronto:Ministry of Community and Social Services, 1985.

Berger, J. *Ways of Seeing* London: B.B.C. [1972] 1988.

Carmichael, S. and C. Hamilton. *Black Power: The Politics of Liberation in America* New York: Routledge, 1967.

Carman, A. and H. Moody. *Working Women* New York: Harper and Row, 1985.

Cashmore, E. and E. McLaughlin, eds. *Out of Order? Policing Black People*. London: Routledge, 1991.

Chesney- Lind, M. "Girls' Crime and Woman's Place: Toward a Feminist Model of Female Delinquency." In J.Sullivan and J.L. Victor, eds. *Criminal Justice 92/93*, Gulford, Conn.:Dushkin, 1992.

Chesney-Lind, M. and R. Sheldon. *Girls, Delinquency and Juvenile Justice*. Belmont: Brooks/Cole, 1992.

Clark, L. and D. Lewis. *Rape: The Price of Coercive Sexuality*. Toronto: Women's Press, 1977.

Cott, N. *The Grounding of Modern Feminism*. New Haven: Yale University Press, 1987.

Crew, K. "Sex Differences in Criminal Sentencing: Chivalry or Patriarchy?" *Justice Quarterly* 8(March, 1991) 1:60-83.

Currie, D. "Female Criminality: A Crisis in Feminist Theory." In B. Maclean, ed. *Political Economy of Crime* Scarborough: Prentice-Hall, 1986.

Currie, D. and M. Kline. "Challenging Privilege: Women, Knowledge and Feminist Struggles." *Journal of Human Justice* 2 (Spring, 1991): 2.

Cusson, M. *Why Delinquency?* Toronto: University of Toronto Press, 1983.

Dixon, Angela. "Going Home: Cash, Control, and Connections in the World of Prostitution." Unpublished paper, Toronto: University of Toronto, 1989.

Dobash, R. E. and R. P. Dobash. *Violence Against Wives: A Case Against Patriarchy.* New York: Free Press, 1979.

Effron, E. *The News Twisters.* Los Angeles: Nash, 1971.

Eisenstein, H. *Contemporary Feminist Thought.* Boston: GK Hall, 1983.

Erez, E. "Gender Rehabilitation and Probation Decisions." *Criminology* 27 (1989) no.2:307-327.

Farell, R. "Materialism and the Adequacy of Self," Unpublished paper, Department of Sociology, York University, 1989.

Fontana, A. "The Stigma of Growing Old: Or Ponce de Leon is Alive and Well and Lives in Leisure Haven, USA." In J. Douglas, ed. *Sociology of Deviance.* Boston: Allyn and Bacon, 1984.

Foucault, M. *Discipline and Punish.* New York: Vintage, 1977.

Foucault, M. *History of Sexuality* V.I. New York: Vintage, 1980.

Freeman, M. D. "Legal Ideologies, Patriarchal Ideologies and Domestic Violence: A Case Study of the English Legal System." In S. Spitzer and R. Simon, eds. *Research in Law, Deviance and Social Control: A Research Annual.* London: J.A.I. Press, 1982.

French, M. *The War Against Women.* New York: Ballantine, 1992.

Glaser, B. and A. Strauss. *The Discovery of Grounded Theory.* Chicago: Aldine, 1967.

Habermas, J. *Theory and Practice.* London: Heinemann Educational Books, 1974.

Hall, S. "The Whites of their Eyes: Racist Ideologies and the Media." In G. Bridges and R. Brunt, eds. *Silver Linings: Some Strategies for the Eighties.* London: Lawrence and Withart, 1981.

Harris, M. *The Dilly Boys.* London: Groom Helm, 1973.

Harris, O. "Households as Natural Units." In K. Young, C. Wolkowitz and R. McCullagh, eds. *Of Marriage and the Market.* London: C. S. E. Books, 1981.

Harris, O. and K. Young. "Engendered Structures: Some Problems in the Analysis of Reproduction." In J. Kahn and J. Llobera, eds) *The Anthropology of Pre-Capitalist Societies*. London: Macmillan, 1981.

Hartmann, H. "Capitalism, Patriarchy and Job Segregation by Sex." In Z. Eisenstein, ed. *Capitalist Patriarchy and the Case for Socialist Feminism* New York: Monthly Review Press, 1979.

Irigaray, L. "The Power of Discourse," *This Sex Is Not One*. Ithaca: Cornell University Press, 1985.

Israel, J. *Alienation From Marx to Modern Sociology*. Boston: Allyn and Bacon, 1971.

Jackson, E. "Street Kids: Nobody's Priority," *Body Politic*. December 1981:7.

King, M. L. Jr. *Why We Can't Wait*. New York: Harper and Row, 1964.

Leavitt, R. *Peacable Primates and Gentle People*. New York: Harper and Row, 1976

Linedecker, C. *Children in Chains*. Boston: Little, Brown, 1981.

Lines, R. "Dare To Struggle.". In K. McCormick and L. A. Visano, eds. *Canadian Penology*. Toronto: Canadian Scholars' Press, 1992.

Lines, R. "On The Prowl." Graduate paper submitted for Sociology of Resistance, York University, North York, 1992.

Lips, H. *Women, Men and Power*. California: Mayfield Publishing, 1991.

Lloyd, R. *Playland*. London: Blond and Briggs Loyd, 1977.

Lowman, J. Vancouver Field Study of Prostitution Working Papers on Pornography and Prostitution Report No. 8. Ottawa: Department of Justice, 1984.

Luxton, M. "Housework" *Canadian Dimension* 12, no. 7 (1978).

Lyotard, J. F. *The Post-modern Condition*.Translated By G. Bennington and B. Massumi. Minneapolis: University of Minnesota, 1984.

Mackie, M. *Constructing Women and Men*. Toronto: Holt, Rinehart and Winston, 1987.

MacKinnon, C. "Feminism, Marxism, Method and the State: An Agenda for Theory." *Signs: Journal of Women in Culture and Society* 7, no. 3:515-544 (1982).

MacKinnon,C. *Feminism Unmodified*. Cambridge: Harvard University Press, 1987.

Malcolm, X. *By Any Means Necessary*. Edited By G. Breitman. New York: Pathfinders, 1970.

Massey, D.S. and N.A. Denton. *American Apartheid: Segregation and the Making of the Underclass*. Cambridge: Harvard University Press, 1993.

McLaren, P. "Predatory Culture and the Politics of Education." Fall vol 1 no. 3 *Cultural Studies Times* (1995):7

Mclntosh, M. "The State and the Oppression of Women." In A. Kuhn and A. Wolpe, eds. *Feminism and Materialism: Women and Modes of Production*. London: Routledge and Kegan Paul, 1978.

McPhersen, B. *Aging As A Social Force*. Toronto: Butterworths, 1983.

NAACP. "Beyond King: An NAACP Report on Police Conduct and Community Relations." *Report*. Baltimore: NAACP, 1993 (April).

Ollman, B. *Alienation*. Cambridge: Cambridge University Press, 1976.

Pollack, O. *The Criminality of Women*. New York: A.S. Barnes, 1961.

Rowbotham, S. "Women's Consciousness, Men's World." In R. Gottlieb, ed. *An Anthology of Westerm Marxism* New York: Oxford University Press, 1989.

Schur, E. *The Politics of Deviance*. Englewood Cliffs: Prentice-Hal, 1980.

Sheehy, G. *Hustling* New York: Delacorte, 1971.

Smart, C. *Women, Crime and Criminology: A Feminist Critique*. London: Routledge and Kegan Paul, 1976.

Smart, C. "Law and the Control of Women's Sexuality: The Case of the 1950s." In B. Hutter and G. Williams, eds. *Controlling Women: The Normal and the Deviant*. London: Croom Helm, 1981.

Smith, D. "Women's Perspective as a Radical Critique of Sociology." *Sociological Inquiry* 44(1)(1973): 7-13.

Smith, D. *Everyday World as Problematic*. Toronto:University of Toronto Press, 1987.

Smith, D. *Conceptual Practices of Power*. Toronto:University of Toronto Press, 1988.

Smith, D. *Texts, Facts and Femininity: Exploring the Relations of Ruling*. NewYork: Routledge, 1990.

Stanko, E. "Would You Believe This Woman?" In N. Hahn Raffer and E. Stanko, eds. *Judge, Lawyer, Victim, Thief*. Boston: Northeastern University Press, 1985

Visano, L. A. "Tramps, Tricks and Trouble: Street Transients and Their Controls." In T. Fleming and L. A. Visano, eds. *Deviant Designations*. Toronto: Butterworth, 1983.

Visano, L. A. *This Idle Trade*. Concord: Vita Sana, 1987.

Visano, L. A. "The Socialization of Street Kids." In N. Mandell, ed. *Sociological Studies of Child Development*, J.A.I. Press, 1990.

Visano, L. A. "Crime as a Commodity: Police Use of Informers." *Journal of Human Justice* (Autumn), 2,1(1990b): pp.105-114.

Visano, L.A."The Impact of Age on Paid Sexual Encounters." In J.A.Lee, ed. *Gay Midlife and Maturity* New York: Harrington Press, 1991.

Visher, C. "Gender, Police Arrest Decisions and Notions of Chivalry." *Criminology* 21(1983): 5-28.

Wax, M. "Paradoxes of Consent to the Practice of Fieldwork." *Social Problems* 27 (February 1990) 3.

Weinstein, C and E. Cummins. "The Crime of Punishment at Pelican Bay Maximum Security Prison." *Covert Action* Summer, 45 (1993):38-45.

Weisberg, D. *Children of the Night*. Lexington: DC Heath, 1985.

Williams, P. *The Alchemy of Race and Rights: Diary of A Law Professor*. Cambridge: Harvard University, 1991.

Boston Globe, 3,03,1990.

Washington Post, 27,02,1990: A3.

CHAPTER 1

Introduction

Arlene was thirteen years of age when she first arrived on the street and turned her first trick. Her first trick entailed performing an oral sex act on a male for $40.00. Her arrival on the street and her emersion into prostitution changed her life significantly and moved her to a lifestyle that engenders much violence, degradation and exploitation. Arlene discloses:

> I had just turned thirteen when me and Karen ran.... We got to Montreal when we met Jason. We didn't have a cent or anything between us, but Jason looked after us. We got stoned with Jason the first night and I think we stayed stoned for at least a week. Karen went off with another guy. ... Jason kept introducing me to prostitutes and players and everyone who was playing the game [prostitution]. We needed the money and I loved Jason at the time, so I agreed to turn a couple of tricks so it would help us out a little. I worked in Montreal, Toronto, Buffalo, Philadelphia and oh hell it seemed like everywhere.... Things started going bad when Jason started beating me up because I wasn't making enough money. Things changed after I got beat up and raped by a bad date. I was beaten so bad that I had to stay in the hospital for two weeks, even my jaw was broken, and you know that Jason didn't come and visit me once. He said that the police were watching the hospital. That was a bunch of crap, but I ended up getting off the street a few weeks after that.
>
> *Interview: Fourteen-year-old: February 2, 1991*

The chapters of this book are concerned with utilizing applied sociological principles and practices to explore and make sense of the social site of juvenile prostitution. Sociological assessment of social phenomena allows for an enhanced level of understanding of various social sites. Sociology, being the study of social phenomenon and its relationship with social institutions and the social actors therein, facilitates a greater awareness of our everyday lives. Sociological methods of inquiry, informed by sociological theory, stimulate assessments and explanations of our various social worlds. Sociology invites individuals to make sense of the apparent non-sense, to become keen observers of the passing social scene, to move beyond our gaze, to challenge our favourite ways of seeing and thinking, and to invoke a critical analysis of our social realities. Sociology provides opportunities to make sense of our social environments. This book incorporates sociological principles and methodology to allow the reader to understand a social site that is prominent in most urban centres in Canada and in the United States.

This monograph is presented in the format of a sociological exploratory study that examines the interactions between male street sex trade managers (street pimps) and female street sex trade workers (street prostitutes). The specific aim of this examination is to provide an extended, applied, conceptual analysis of the pimp-prostitute relationship. There have been numerous studies and much research on prostitution, but there has been very limited examination of the role that pimps play in the "prostitution scene." Many reports on prostitution vaguely mention the involvement of pimps and often fail to move their examination beyond cursory comments regarding their role. Therefore, pimps are often portrayed as secondary actors in street prostitution subculture.

Some reports describe the pimp-prostitute relationship as one of "mutual functional interdependence." This "mutual functional model" suggests that pimps play a role in assisting and providing necessary services to prostitutes. Prostitutes are often portrayed as entrepreneurs, and pimps are often dismissed as assistants in many studies of street prostitutes. It is asserted in this text that these accounts do not accurately depict or describe how central the pimp's role is manifest within street prostitution subculture. This examination provides a much needed critical analysis of the role that pimps play in the recruitment, the training and the compelling of women to work as prostitutes. Karen and Beth report the role of their pimp respectively:

> Billy did everything for me, I mean he turned me out and made sure I was safe on the street, but at the time he was more than that, I mean I was in love with him... He was good to me

until I started getting mad about the other girls that he was spending more of his time with. That's when he started hitting me and stuff. Our relationship changed a lot then. He started forcing me to work and wouldn't let me come in until I earned $700.00 a night. At first he helped me out a lot, then he just beat me for no reason.

Interview: Fifteen-year-old:January 10, 1990

Cecil picked me up at the pinball place and I immediately fell in love with him. He was so affectionate and loving. We made love the first night and we partied together for five or six days. Cecil kept introducing me to a bunch of his friends who were playing the game, but he said I was too special for the streets.... It turned out that he had some plans for me to work as a prostitute for people who were involved in gambling houses and stuff. At first I was making a lot of money and we were living the 'high life,' literally, we were stoned much of the time. Cecil would take me to the gambling houses and pick me up, he looked after me well.... I didn't really get out of prostitution until Cecil got arrested and I went to the group home.

Interview: Fifteen-year-old: April 12, 1989

This inquiry details that pimps are, indeed, significant primary actors who are involved in producing and reproducing the subculture of street prostitution. Therefore, this work focuses directly on the role that pimps play in promoting and regenerating street prostitution.

This analysis develops and facilitates a qualitative methodological inquiry into the pimp-prostitute relationship. Specifically, elements of qualitative analysis are exercised throughout this study to demonstrate the methodological process of qualitative approaches to understanding social phenomena. A social typology of adolescent prostitutes is generated to assess emergent social research that attempts to identify characteristics of juvenile prostitution. This examination includes the analysis of determining the role of pimps and how central the pimp's role remains in the prostitute's life. Elements of the role and function of pimps to be examined include the claim of providing protection, the imagery involved, the established hierarchy within the spectrum of pimping and a subcultural social typology of pimps. The procurement methods that pimps employ and the characteristics of the relationship that develop will disclose the level of vulnerability and dependence, the gender relations, the psychological coercion, the training, the application of the trade, the working relations, the violence and abduction and the consequences of this exposure. Emergent sociological approaches are imposed that assess the assumption of this pimp-prostitute relationship as one of "mutual functional interdependence" and argues for an alternative model. This alternative model maintains that the pimp-prostitute relationship is exploitive, degrading and often results in various levels of violence being inflicted on women.

This sociological inquiry is undertaken to attract students, academics and practitioners from various disciplines and occupations who have an interest in the "applied social sciences" within a "qualitative context." This practical application of qualitative methods allows students, sociologists, criminologists, social psychologists, child-youth workers, social workers, court workers, law enforcement officials and a general readership to explore a street subculture that exists in many urban centres. Great care has been taken to present this material in a manner that is readable and understandable. This descriptive account of the pimp-prostitute relationship serves to immerse the reader in a subculture that is complex and poorly understood. This work facilitates an eclectic approach of practical, legal and academic findings and research to assist readers in obtaining a greater understanding of this prominent social site.

Much of the data utilized within this effort were accessible because of significant policy changes and program development over the last twelve years in many urban centres across Canada and the United States. Significant developments have been made in the method of delivery of child-care and police services. The magnitude of the juvenile prostitution problem has demanded, for the most part, that child-care and police representatives make significant changes in enforcement philosophy and approaches. These policy changes have resulted in an increase of state apprehension and retention of children, which has resulted in significant increases in disclosure of information from these children and adolescents involved in prostitution. It is due to these policy changes and program developments that data were generated and, therefore, this exploratory study was made possible. Although not every region invoked changes in policy and strategy, a significant number have made changes and are continuing to develop programs that will meet the needs of this specialized group of adolescents in crisis. These changes in policy are articulated within this study to highlight the social context in which the data were collected. Furthermore, highlighting these changes in policy serves to illustrate that good social policy can, in many circumstances, be effective in addressing societal problems.

Preliminary perusal of the available data illustrates that children as young as ten years of age are exchanging sexual acts for money in many urban centres. The estimated number of children employed as sex trade workers ranges on any given day from 10,000 on the streets of Canada to 100,000 on American streets. Of course, there are problematic features of gathering reliable statistical assessments of the numbers of children and adolescents working as prostitutes. However, most officials working in the child-care services recognize that juvenile prostitution has become a reality on the social landscape in most urban jurisdictions.

Although quantitative analysis of the scope of this social problem provides limited disclosure, social and legal research indicates that each year hundreds of children are experiencing severe social conditions and circumstances. The results of these dysfunctional social conditions are that a significant number of children eventually find themselves working as street prostitutes. The data demonstrate that a significant number of children are "falling through the cracks" of child welfare systems. Many of the children are victims of abuse at home and are further victimized by inadequate school and child welfare responses. Heather and Alana both report their experiences at home, school and with child care authorities respectively by disclosing:

> Things were not going very well at home. After dad died, mom just kept drinking and was always going out with idiots. One of her boyfriends raped me and that's when I left home the first time.... When they sent me back home, the youth workers told my teachers that I was involved in prostitution, even though at that time I wasn't. My teachers and everybody at school treated me like crap and they kept saying things like the 'Happy Hooker'.... I ran from home after a few days but got caught again and then they put me in a group home. That was a disaster, the workers kept me way from the other kids because they said that I was a hooker and likely had AIDS...I think I lasted there for two days before I ran again. They didn't catch me again for eight months.
>
> *Interview: Fifteen-year-old: May 10, 1990*

> I wasn't getting along at home or at school. I got suspended twice for drinking on school grounds. I couldn't stay at home any longer, it was so crazy I had to leave. I got caught and they put me in a group home, what a joke. They kept thinking

> I was going to take other kids with me when I ran. I couldn't
> stay at the group home, like they were so fixated on the
> prostitution thing that they made it worse than it was.... At
> least on the street I could do what I wanted to do.
>
> *Interview: Sixteen-year-old: December 3, 1989*

A significant number of these displaced and disenfranchised children run to the streets only to be victimized further by the street subculture.

The violent realities of life on the street are often expressed with reckless abandonment and disregard for the lives of these vulnerable children and adolescents. Reports of street prostitutes being brutalized by "bad dates" (customers) or victimized by pimps are very common within this street subculture. A case study of one fifteen-year-old victim of a "bad date" reveals that she was taken to the hospital after she reported being sexually assaulted by two men in a van. She required over 190 stitches on her thigh to close a knife wound inflicted by one of the assailants. The victim's eyes were swollen shut and her cheek bone and collar bone were broken. She had been dropped in a ditch by the suspects after they had physically and sexually assaulted her. Another example of the violent expression of the street is captured in a case study of a fourteen-year-old victim who had been brutally assaulted by a pimp. The pimp had taken a knife and carved his initials, "TJ," into her stomach. He then proceeded to beat her with a coat hanger (pimp stick). He continued with his assault, broke her nose, cheek bone and fractured four of her ribs. This pimp suspected that she had talked to another pimp; therefore, in his view, she deserved this punishment. Incidents such as these are indeed commonplace in many cities, with varying degrees of violence being inflicted upon children and adolescents involved in prostitution.

Numerous urban centres have invoked various programs and policies to address this social problem. Some cities have developed juvenile task forces that specialize in addressing the needs of juvenile prostitutes. These developments can be seen as incremental because of the increased awareness and concern by community members and politicians regarding juvenile prostitution and the violence surrounding this street subculture. A number of social service agencies that handle children and adolescents are reporting significant increases in the number of women under eighteen years of age, most being runaways, becoming involved in the life of prostitution. This specialization and awareness of the social site of juvenile prostitution has forced some social service agencies to mandate a philosophical shift. This philosophical understanding or perspective to view the "child as victim" has in some jurisdictions provided a clear picture of how the police and other social service agencies need to respond to the "juvenile prostitution problem." Several regions have advocated for a holistic approach to this emergent problem. Many child-care agencies, over the last several years, have been able to agree on a path that would maximize existing services and incorporate new initiatives to provide efficient and necessary crisis intervention and support for children involved in prostitution.

Program initiatives over the last twelve years have detailed that the police and child-care officials work very closely with a shared mandate in order to be successful in meeting the needs of juvenile prostitutes. Numerous agencies have invoked a mandate under existing child welfare legislation to apprehend children involved in prostitution, and therefore deemed to be at risk and in need of protection. The children are usually taken to a designated place of safety for crisis intervention and counselling. For the most part, these initiatives have resulted in crisis intervention being conducted by specially trained child-youth workers, social workers and police officers. The care and support that these specialized workers are able to provide for the children has, in numerous cases, resulted in an alarming rate of disclosure by many children as to how they found themselves involved in prostitution. This disclosure often details much about an abusive home life, the resulting diminished school and social environments and the child's attempt to exile herself from such negative environmental conditions.

The data collected from these children demonstrate that these children are not running to the streets, but, in most cases, are indeed running from an abusive situation at home. The street often seems to be the only perceived option at the time. The disclosure by these women illustrates that most of them are not running away from their residences with any intention of becoming involved in prostitution. It is most evident that when these young women arrive in urban centres they are being procured into a life of prostitution. This procurement into prostitution is usually operationalized by several adult organizers, namely pimps, who appear to be very active in most major urban centres.

Agencies also reported that "turf wars" and a greater incidence of "jacking up" (robbing) prostitutes of their "trap" (money) was occurring on the "stroll" (street) in many regions. These incidents appeared to force pimps to attend to the "stroll" to ensure that their interests were being maintained. Moreover, the incidence of pimps having to operate openly on the streets, in shopping malls and in video arcades resulted in a growing incidence of young adolescents coming into direct contact with pimps and, therefore, increasing the numbers being procured into prostitution. This influx of pimps aggressively procuring young women into prostitution was seen by some child-care and police officials as one of the many factors that needed to be addressed within the holistic approach of preventing juvenile prostitution. It was with this intention to utilize legal sanctions against these adult organizers of juvenile prostitutes that child-care and police agencies were able to specialize and become involved in the investigation of pimps and their role in juvenile prostitution.

This specialization and subsequent greater understanding of all the contributing factors of juvenile prostitution has permitted the generation of data and an awareness that reveals all significant social actors involved in this social site. It further reveals that juvenile prostitutes are not fallen women, sluts or whores but are, in fact, our children. It is obvious that child-care and police agencies are competing for our children on the streets—the competitors are the pimps. The pimps have developed and provide a complete system of outreach, intake, on-the-job training, peer support, protection and work incentives for young women. Can our child-care agencies compete with the opportunities that are provided by pimps? This question and others will be forthcoming in this text.

The definition of "pimp" and "prostitute" employed within the framework of this study is determined from the current legal interpretation of the legislation contained in the Criminal Code of Canada. Section 212. (1),(2),(3) of the Criminal Code is commonly called the "pimp legislation" within the legal community and outlines eleven offences that upon conviction would indeed label one as a pimp. Three of the offences are listed here to provide a general definition and understanding of the legal concept of a pimp. Greenspan (1994:207) outlines Section 212.(1) of the Criminal Code:

> Every one who:
> (d) procures or attempts to procure a person to become, whether in or out of Canada, a prostitute,
> (h) for the purpose of gain, exercises control, direction or influence over the movements of a person in such a manner as to show that he is aiding, abetting or compelling that person to engage in or carry on prostitution with any person or generally,
> (j) lives wholly or in part on the avails of prostitution of another person
> is guilty of an indictable offence and liable to imprisonment for a term not exceeding ten years.

The definition of "prostitute" utilized within this study is drawn from the current legal interpretation of case law. A prostitute is defined as "one who completes sex acts in exchange for money or goods." These definitions are offered to clarify how these terms are understood within a legal context. It is within this legal context that the terms pimp and prostitute are utilized in this examination.

The dynamics of the pimp-prostitute relationship are determined by the methods that pimps select to procure and exercise control of women for the purposes of prostitution. The method that pimps select to procure and exercise control is directly dependent on the age and the level of vulnerability of the women. Subsequently, the nature of the relationship varies. This work asserts that the dynamics of this interaction between pimps and prostitutes are not those of mutual functional interdependence, but ones in which pimps exhort various levels of exploitation, degradation, dominance and manipulation regardless of what method of procurement and control they choose to invoke.

This introductory chapter informs the reader of the pervasive problem of adolescent prostitution that continues to flourish in many Canadian and American cities. This issue has and continues to provoke much emotional response, concern and even anger from many people who are aware of this social crisis. Further analysis is needed to fully appreciate and understand this social site. Specifically, preventive and interventional measures cannot be effectively operationalized without a complete understanding of the many "actors" and their "roles" within this street subculture. This chapter serves to "map out" exactly where this text takes the reader as one embarks upon this exploration of the games pimps play.

In the following chapters, analyses of data, self-reports, court transcripts and field observations are utilized to examine the sociological considerations of the street sex trade. Chapter Two details the many methodological concerns and realizations of advancing a qualitative study of a social site that vehemently makes itself inaccessible to "outsiders." Chapter Three highlights a social typology of juvenile prostitutes by providing an analysis of current data that identifies the characteristics of those involved in juvenile prostitution. In Chapter Four, the seduction method of procurement is outlined to provide a greater understanding of this most effective strategy utilized by pimps to coerce women into prostitution.

The compelling features of the pimp's systematic methods of procurement are again highlighted in Chapter Five, but with direct analysis of the stratagem method of procurement. Chapter Six examines the training process to which women are subjected to in order to "learn the game." Chapter Seven follows the methods of procurement to reveal the movement towards abductions and the levels of gratuitous violence that are often inflicted upon prostitutes. It also reveals the consequences of this exploitation on those who have witnessed or become victims of physical violence.

Chapter Eight moves to provide a closer critique of the pimp's role and function to reveal how pimps generate employment strategies by monopolizing on violence. This chapter highlights the imagery and hierarchical structures of pimps and discloses cultural implications that are generated through imagery and stereotypes. It also develops a subcultural social typology of pimps to pull together some of their common qualities, similarities and disparities.

Chapter Nine moves to explore the police and social services responses to the street sex trade. The enforcement of pimp legislation is examined to reveal a much needed police and social services philosophical shift in responses to this social site. Lastly, the concluding chapter provides theoretical sociological approaches and perspectives to petition greater understanding of this social site and to clarify the implications bestowed on a woman who becomes involved in prostitution.

CHAPTER 2

Methodological Issues:
Researching "The Game"

Introduction

The primary research aim of this exploratory study, as detailed in the introductory chapter, is to investigate the interactions between male sex trade managers (street pimps) and female sex trade workers (street prostitutes). Particularly, this qualitative study is designed to provide an extended conceptual analysis of the pimp-prostitute relationship. This qualitative effort is directed at approximating valid knowledge regarding the role of pimps and how central the pimp's role remains in the prostitute's life. In other words, the overall goal of this methodology is to collect the richest possible data to advance an inquiry into the pimp-prostitute relationship. This goal is realized by conducting a comprehensive review of research and related literature, content analyses of secondary sources, field observations and intensive interviews with respondents participating in street prostitution. The merging of this data, within this methodological construct, informs the thesis of this text.

The objective of this chapter is to highlight the instrumental factors of making sense of and documenting social phenomena. Many ethnographers of social intercourse proudly display the results of their observations and field work but often do not provide any commentary on how they obtained their results. This denial of methodological discourse condemns the reader to speculate about methodological concerns and creditability. Furthermore, this denial maintains a fractured portrait of the sociological inquiry process. Methodological design and inception is not just something but is everything in conducting social analysis. The many strengths and weaknesses of methodological inquiry must be disclosed in order to provide the reader with a complete picture of sociological analysis; otherwise, the reader is kept in a state of ignorance or disillusionment about the process of sociological inquiry and is compelled to accept the findings without critical inspection. This chapter reveals how this research on the social phenomena of street prostitution was administered and "made sense of." Moreover, this chapter provides an applied, in-depth view and appreciation of the struggle and complexities of sociological research.

Methodological Process

Sociology, as a discipline, has developed a set of methods for determining the cause and effects of relations in our social lives. Isolating and understanding social relations or phenomena usually begin with some sort of observation made by the sociologist of some interesting social aspect, ritual, act or site. Sociologists usually wish to move these observations beyond mere speculation to learn more about our social world. These speculations could be classified as casual observations or generalizations about the social event that has been witnessed. However, observations are only generalizations and obviously cannot be offered as being grounded in any type of empirical measurement or offering any sociological conclusions about the phenomena. A social scientist will now need to isolate further exactly what is to be studied and therefore measured. This process often takes on the form of hypothesis generation. The struggle for the social scientists often begins here in developing and administering the appropriate measurement devices to capture and make sense of the social phenomena. Social scientists must design and administer a systematic process to allow scientific measurement of the social site in order to test the hypothesis.

The research design and administration of methodology is the procedure for collecting and interpreting data with the assumption that this analysis will assist in the comprehension of our social lives. Research design and administration can take many forms. Quantitative analysis principles could be utilized that would incorporate the use of surveys, experimental designs, questionnaires, panel studies and phone surveys. Qualitative analysis may also be conducted that would include such methods as participant observation, natural setting experiments, covert observational studies, intensive interviewing and field observations. Quantitative analysis allows access to a significant number of respondents but often is restrictive in the substantive, in-depth information that one can elicit. Qualitative analysis permits access to a small number of respondents but facilitates an in-depth probing into the social world of the respondent. The sociologist will need to select the methodological process that will demonstrate empirically that the methods are valid and reliable.

Research results are no better than the methods by which they are obtained; therefore, methodological development must be seen as pertinent to the study of social phenomena. The initial sensing of a problem and the application of research methods result in the problem of choosing the appropriate methods of sociological measurement. Sociology is the study of systems of social action and of their interrelations. The developing of sociological explanations to interpret these relationships involves rigorous investigations of social phenomena. Sociology faces all of the problems that are common to the behaviourial sciences generally in regard to establishing appropriate methods of measurement. Most sociologists are keenly aware of the hypothetical nature of many of the variables which they must measure. A hypothetical construct is something that is believed to exist because the effect attributed to it is observable, even though the phenomenon itself cannot be, or at least, has not been directly observed (Lasswell, 1974:147).

The research process is the overall method of scientific activity in which sociologists engage in order to "make sense of the non-sense." The methodological principle adhered to within this exploration is the interactionist perspective. The interactionist perspective allows the researcher to move the research process to both testing theories and to having them represent a never-ending interaction between empirical research and theoretical work.

Visano (1987) suggests that the sociological process is facilitated through a never-ending interaction between empirical research and theoretical efforts. As an endowment to theoretical activity, Visano (1987:44-45) notes that the interactionist perspective demonstrates the various stages of the research process and that this theoretical assumption must play a prominent role in empirical investigations. Visano (1987: 44-45) recognizes that the "social" is developed and realized by the processes in which the actors interpret and assign meanings to their everyday experiences. The process of the everyday is being constructed and reconstructed in that social action and interaction are changing and developing phenomena that are not static experiences. If one is to fully understand social phenomena, one must utilize this interactionist pattern in order to capture and document the nature of the process and structure of social phenomena. The research process, under this format, permits flexibility and adaptability to each research site or condition and is conducive both to testing theories and constructing them.

This flexible and adaptable methodological practice facilitates the examination of the interconnectedness of the social organization of street prostitution. By utilizing both formats it maximizes the understanding of this site and moves beyond rigid socio-methodological concepts in order to facilitate a methodology that adapts itself to the social phenomena under study. The methodology practiced within this exploratory study utilizes both the "research-then-theory" format and the "theory-then-research" format. Therefore, empirical data and generalizations or observational reports generate theories, and those theories generate researchable problems to inform the thesis of this study. The forthcoming data are utilized to maximize validity in describing an accurate approximation of the world of pimping.

Review of Academic Work and Data: Secondary Data Sources

Secondary data sources are a major research resource used by most sociologists. These sources include literature and data from published and unpublished academic works, statistical reports, court transcripts and statements given to the police. Other sources such as the notebooks of police officers will be utilized. The scholarships and the secondary data sources are included within this explanation of methodological practices to highlight the relevance and impact that these sources have on collecting empirical data and selecting theoretical application.

The scholarships are indeed pertinent to this methodology as they inform, guide and often direct the researcher to the data. The scholarships are an important factor within this methodology and are expressed throughout this study. Much of the literature and scholarships on street prostitution are used to corroborate the observational data. Furthermore, the existing data often demonstrate a limited availability and completeness of data, and, therefore, direct the researcher to explore areas that seem to be lacking original empirical investigation. Secondary data sources are represented in many other forms within this text. Content analysis of task force reports, public inquiries submissions, public commissions and other literature that represent inspection of street prostitution are invaluable sources that ground this text. Content analysis of the above noted sources provides a diverse range of fertile data that prominently inform this inquiry.

Participant Observation:
The Naturalistic Tradition

The field observations conducted within this effort espouse "participant observation" methodology. Utilizing participant observation methodology allows researchers to "make sense" of situations and structures from the "insider's view." This involves attempting to discover the viewpoint of the actors involved in the unfolding phenomena and their relationship with the total social institution, social system or subculture. Since observations are made over time, social processes can be observed; the formation, crystallization and disillusionment of subcultural attitudes are made visible. The interrelationship between individuals and parts of the subculture leads the researcher to an enhanced level of understanding of the social phenomenon being studied. Participant observational methods facilitate original and authentic enlightenment about the social phenomena being investigated. This authentic and original location to the social existence prepares the researcher to develop theoretical manifestations.

Visano, in his work on street prostitution, clearly articulates his reliance on participant observation as a satisfactory field observational methodology. Visano (1987:45-46) asserts that participational observation facilitates the methodological charge of interactionism by permitting the researcher to obtain first-hand experience and knowledge about the everyday life of the actors and the interrelatedness with their social world. The emersion of the researcher into the social world of the actors enables the researcher to document the social reality of the actors and to develop conceptual apportionments from the observational data. The participant observation model moves sociological research beyond the "keyhole observer" (Garfinkle, 1967) methodology and immerses the researcher into the social world of the subjects.

Participant observation facilitates the lowering or removing of the informational barriers that are often in place when observing a research site from a distance or from the "outside looking in." As Goffman (1961:ix-x) points out:

> Any group of persons—prisoners, primitives, pilots, or patients—develops a life of their own that becomes meaningful, reasonable and normal once you get close to it ... and a good way to learn about any of these worlds is to submit oneself in the company of the members to the daily round of petty contingencies to which they are subject.

Visano (1987:46) also notes that "as a methodology, participant observation takes into account the inner as well as the outer perspectives of the subjects." Becker and Geer (1970:133) support the ability of participant observers to capture the "everyday circumstances" of the subjects by noting that this method allows observers to participate in the day-to-day activities of people under study. Observing things, listening to what is being said, talking to and questioning people about their social reality all become part of the participant observer's attempt to capture the inner perspective. When researchers immerse themselves into the everyday social world of the subjects, they stand to gain the trust and confidence of the actors within the site under study. This level of trust and confidence will facilitate the "naturalism tradition" of minimizing the presupposition when the researcher enters the "everyday life" of the actors. By embracing naturalism, the researcher minimizes any disruption or interference that his or her presence could create with the natural course of events. This ensures that the actors provide the researcher with honest answers to the questions and do not conceal important activities from view.

Another important factor in adopting this methodology is that it is conducive to permitting access to difficult or closed social settings. The study of the organization of prostitution lends itself to the methods of "naturalistic research" because of the subcultural barriers that are in place. The adoption of this methodology allows the researcher to view the social organization of prostitution as it is "phenomenally experienced by actors in their natural environment"(Visano, 1987:47). Other research methods such as surveys, inquiries, experimental designs and secondary data studies often fall short of capturing appropriate approximations or in-depth analyses of the "everyday life" of the actors within street prostitution. Other methodological designs are often problematic when encountered by "closed social settings" or the "code of silence" that is often manifest by the actors engaged in prostitution. This "code of silence" generates much suspicion, protectionism, fear and usually outright "denial of entry" into this research site. The "them" and "us" subcultural attitude that is veraciously generated, defended and indoctrinated within the prostitution environment limits the effectiveness and access of most research methods but provides challenging accounts for the naturalistic tradition. By embracing the naturalistic tradition, the researcher can gain access to this site and spend time with the actors on their "turf" (Visano, 1987:47), obtain the trust and confidence of the actors and, therefore, obtain the richest, most reflective data possible that captures the social organization of prostitution.

Researcher's Role

The "proper" research role is a methodological issue that centres on the degree to which field workers should participate within the studied scene. Although research roles can be clearly defined within most research efforts, these roles become somewhat problematic within the context of this study of the social organization of prostitution. The researcher was a sworn police officer during much of the participant observational period, thus often competing with personal attitudes and aspiring professional interests. Visano (1987:48) notes that a researcher must be able to adapt to different roles while conducting participant observational work by suggesting that he or she is indeed required to play a role that is not only comfortable enough for the subjects to accept but also comfortable enough for the researcher. Also under consideration, as highlighted by Visano (1987), is a role that allows the movement towards achieving greater acceptance and facilitating greater access to the "intimate accounts" of the lives of the subjects. The researcher role must also, as Visano (1987) points out, be versatile enough to permit the researcher to observe the social site while being able to "record, compare and analyze." Researcher roles may therefore move back and forth from various levels of participation to complete observation.

The scholarships within naturalistic methodology identify the role of a researcher as a field worker who moves back and forth from research subjects to his or her "sociological discipline." The controversy here begins with the acceptability of observational evidence received while the researcher was naive or somewhat uninformed of sociological methodology. The researcher, within this effort, began making informal observations of the street prostitution environment in 1977 when he was sworn in as a police officer. The documented experiences of "making sense" of this street subculture began to take written academic form in 1983 when the researcher completed an introduction to sociology course at the undergraduate level. The researcher's earlier experiences are documented in police memo books and are utilized in this study for content analysis purposes. Further academic development of sociological methodological format provided the researcher with a greater understanding of researcher roles and the connection with academic and ethical expectations of sociological research.

Some academics may argue that the participation observational data obtained in this study is flawed, as the researcher was professionally involved with the research and site causing the analysis to be biased. Speculation of observer bias in the collection of data is not a new issue in methodological sociology. Many teachers of participant observation insist that, at all times and in all situations, the sociologist must attempt to maintain distance and, therefore, objectivity in order to retain observational clarity. The obvious conflict here is between the principles of the naturalistic traditions of research, which demand getting close to the subjects in order to take the "viewpoint" of those whose structured life situation is being studied, and the paradoxical position, which insists that one must remain aloof in order to perceive what is in fact happening. The method of collecting and utilizing the participant observational data in this study is justified by adopting the naturalistic tradition, which projects the positive tradition of "starting where you are" (Lofland and Lofland, 1984:9). Lofland and Lofland (1984:9) cite Everett Hughes's comments of Robert Park, one of the original advocators of naturalist tradition:

> Most of these people [sociology graduate students] didn't have any sociological background.... They didn't come in to become sociologists. They came in to learn something and Park picked up whatever it was in their experience which he could build on.... He took those people and he brought out of them whatever he could find there. And he brought out of them very often something they themselves did not know was there.

Accompanied by academic development, the researcher has progressed through the participant-observer role to utilize the experiences received while serving as a police officer. Moreover, the researcher has, through further academic development, and, in particular, by example of this study, built on the participant-observational data to corroborate the observational findings through intensive interviewing. The transformation of participant-observer roles indeed facilitated further analysis of the observational data. Therefore, the researcher's closeness and professional involvement to the observational site of this study are not viewed as an obstacle or a barrier but as a formula that has promoted and developed this sociological inquiry over several years to disclose a longitudinal "insider's view" of the social organization of prostitution.

Interviews:
Research Participants

Another methodological consideration utilized in this study is the administration of intensive interviews or self-reports with respondents participating in street prostitution. As indicated earlier, the self-reports corroborate the observational data and obtain further detailed material for qualitative analysis. Intensive interview methodology is an instrumental factor in retaining the "insider's view" and thus observational clarity. Lofland and Lofland (1984:13) articulate the interconnectedness of intensive interviewing and participant observation when conducting qualitative research:

> Classic participant observation always involves the interweaving of looking and listening, of watching and asking—and some of that listening and asking may approach or be identical to intensive interviewing. Conversely, intensive interview studies may involve repeated and prolonged contact between researchers and informants, sometimes extending over a period of years, with considerable mutual involvement in personal lives—a characteristic often considered a hallmark of participant observation.... For these reasons, then, we wish to emphasize the mutuality of participant observation and intensive interviewing as the central techniques of the naturalistic investigator.

The intensive interviewing or self-reports are comprised from two substantial sources. These self-reports and participant observations are interwoven within this effort to maximize the quality of the data in order to obtain the actor's perceptions of the social organization of prostitution.

One set of respondents, which is given significant reliance, is derived from interviews with 194 prostitutes from across Canada and the United States. These respondents were as young as twelve years of age and as old as twenty-seven years of age at the time of the interview. One hundred and sixty were under eighteen years of age and the remaining thirty-four were eighteen years of age or older (see Table One for complete age distribution of the respondents). The interviewing process began in 1983 and continued until 1994. The researcher met with many of the respondents on numerous occasions to clarify details and comments and to receive further data on the changing social scene. Most

Table One

Women's Ages and the Number Interviewed (Self-Reports)

Years of Age	Interviewed
12	8
13	12
14	31
15	39
16	43
17	27

Total interviewed under 18 years of age = 160

Women's Ages and the Number Interviewed (Self-Reports)

Years of Age	Interviewed
18	15
19	8
21	4
23	3
24	2
27	2

Total interviewed 18 years of age and over = 34

of the respondents were in the custody of state agencies when these interviews were conducted. Eighty-four eventually gave evidence in the criminal justice system as to the involvement of pimps in their lives. The subsequent court transcripts are utilized to further corroborate the accuracy and reliability of the respondent's information.

The second set of self-reports are from interviews, conversations and court testimony from twenty-eight different men from across Canada and the United States who were involved in pimping activity. These respondents were as young as fifteen years of age and as old as thirty-seven years of age at the time they were interviewed (see Table Two for complete age distribution of respondents). This interviewing process also began in 1983 and concluded in 1993. Again, most of these respondents were also in custody of state agencies at the time

Table Two

Pimps' Ages and the Number Interviewed (Self-Reports)	
Years of Age	Interviewed
15	2
16	1
18	3
21	5
24	4
29	6
33	3
36	2
37	2
Total pimps interviewed = 28	

that they were interviewed. All twenty-eight were eventually charged and convicted of pimp-related criminal offences.

Observational Reports

The observational reports adopted are those observations made in the field, which began in 1983 and continued until 1989. Many of these field observations were conducted in a covert manner while the researcher was conducting police surveillance on the activity of pimps. Some of the field observational data that are utilized were encountered while interviewing pimps and conducting observations of pimps who were engaged in the court process. The observational reports are used to corroborate the self-reports and relevant literature and to offer further analysis of the pimp-prostitute relationship.

Confidentiality of the respondents is of utmost importance, therefore, the identity of the respondents will be withheld. In keeping with the sociological practice of guaranteeing anonymity, the respondents are not identified in order to protect their dignity and to comply with legislative requirements of confidentiality within the various juvenile justice systems. Although many of the names are available on the public records of the criminal and civil courts, it serves no purpose to further stigmatize respondents who, in many cases, have moved on with their lives. Visano (1987:55) points out the obligation to ensure the confidentiality of respondents by suggesting that although social scientists may have an obligation to contribute to knowledge, they also have a duty and responsibility to protect participants in their research. The guarantee of confidentiality within this research effort is directly linked to affording respectability and compassion for the subjects who, all too often, have been the victims of exploitive endeavours.

In conclusion, the methodology naturalized in this text is designed to characterize the social action and interaction that accompanies the social organization of prostitution. An accurate assessment of the interaction and interconnectedness of prostitution, the actors and the emergent relations are fostered by this methodology. The collection of the richest possible data to advance this sociological inquiry and analysis is facilitated by this methodology to reveal the social aspects of the pimp-prostitute relationship.

CHAPTER 3

Juvenile Prostitutes:
A Social Typology

Entrepreneur or Street Survival?

Up until the early 1980s, much social research had been conducted on adult prostitutes; however, very little in-depth analysis had been conducted to disclose the experiences of juveniles who become involved in prostitution. This exploration of the games pimps play begins with an examination of who are the women that pimps engage. A social typology of juvenile prostitutes is offered here to identify the characteristics of those involved in prostitution. This analysis of current data and self-reports identifies some of the common circumstances and experiences of female prostitutes with reference to such dimensions as: background, family composition and characteristics; history of sexual, psychological and physical abuse; level of formal education; age; socioeconomic status; physical and mental health; race; drug usage; and a concluding social typology. Since the early 1980s, an increase in research of this social site has generated data and literature that identify many common characteristics that juvenile prostitutes exhibit and experience.

Background and Family Composition

As pointed out in the introductory chapter, many of the juveniles interviewed for this project disclosed that they were not running to the street to become involved in prostitution, but, in fact, were running from abusive situations at home. Often the street was the only perceived option. This sense of limited options is illustrated in the following comments by Lori and Karen respectively:

> It was really shit at home. It didn't matter what I did, it wasn't right. They drove me fucking crazy. They would search my room and everything. My dad kept accusing me of taking drugs, which was bullshit. Even my grades weren't good enough. I couldn't stay there any more. I had to leave. I didn't know where I was going, but I just had to get out.
>
> *Interview: Thirteen-year-old: April 9, 1991*

> I didn't know anything about the street. I didn't have anything. But when you arrive, you learn fast. You have to or you die. But anything was better than living at home. They had screwed up my head so much I just ran. But I learned everything I needed within a few days. You can learn quick.
>
> *Interview: Fourteen-year-old: February 6, 1989*

The idea of prostitution, in most cases, became a factor for consideration by women after they arrived on the street. These women did not have any original intention of working as prostitutes before leaving their places of abode. This focus is therefore generated on the circumstances that induced them to see the street as a feasible choice.

The data collected reveal that many of the respondents had been involved with various child-youth agencies before their immersion into prostitution. The children and their families, because of dysfunctional circumstances or complete breakdown of the family unit, had been brought to the attention of child-youth agencies. The self-reports disclose that there is a significant projection of escalating events in the child's family life, which subsequently affect their personal life to such intensity as to bring the young person to the attention of child-youth care agencies. The Toronto Street Youth Project Interim Evaluation Report (1986:1) describes newly arrived clients as:

> Lacking basic skills; having low self-esteem; being distrustful of adults; expecting rejection; emotionally younger than their chronological age; impulsive and lacking social judgement. Most have a history of poor school attendance and are behind age expectations in academic skill level. Only 2 percent of the youths had work experience other than prostitution,

79 percent reported drug use, with multiple drug use being the norm, 86 percent were living away from their families at the time of their first admission into the Toronto Street Youth Project.

The battered past of these young people, or some might say "the walking wounded" who are emotionally, psychologically and physically scarred by their own family experiences, makes them indeed ripe candidates for street prostitution. The Toronto Street Youth Project (1986:6) reports recognizing the destructive and vulnerable state of these walking wounded:

> In the majority of cases, the youths got involved in prostitution as a result of their lack of life skills. They remained in it because of a past history of rejection and their low self-esteem... the youth assuming responsibility for providing her own food and shelter, discovers that her lack of work skills leaves her with few options other than prostitution. This activity is encouraged by a pimp who gains an emotional hold over the youth by claiming to care for her. The youth remains in prostitution because the money she earns gives her the feeling that she does have some skills, and hence worth, while the pimp and "street family" provides the acceptance that she has been unable to get elsewhere. In spite of their tough exterior and bravado many youths are conscious of their lack of competence. As a result, they feel inept and expect to be rejected.

The vulnerability and hopelessness of these adolescents tends to be very much a distinguishing characteristic. What is it that has occurred in their lives to have produced such specimens of despondency and self-destruction? The essential point being made here is that young people don't just wake up one morning and say, "Hey, I think I'm going to be a prostitute today," then get dressed and go downtown to acquire the services of a pimp and start turning tricks. The behaviour of these adolescents is an expression of their past and current social environments that incorporates and expresses their earlier family and social turmoil. Subsequently, adolescent females are very vulnerable when they arrive on the street.

In an attempt to test the "vulnerability theory," respondents were questioned about their preparation for street life. The level of vulnerability of

Table Three

Levels of Vulnerabilities

	Levels of Vulnerability			
	High	%	Low	%
Subject: Under 18 yrs = 160	143	89%	17	11%
Subject:18 yrs and older = 34	14	41%	20	59%
Subject Total = 194	157	81%	37	19%

the respondents is one characteristic that stood out. The level of vulnerability is defined in terms of two categories: high levels of vulnerability and low levels of vulnerability. The distinction is determined by the woman's real life circumstances upon arrival on the streets. A high level of vulnerability is characteristic of a woman who arrived in a downtown centre with little money or other resources available to provide adequate shelter, food, clothing or other essential necessities of life. Low level of vulnerability would be those women who have enough money and resources available to them to provide some adequate shelter, food, clothes and other essential necessities of life. This classification does not capture or estimate any levels of emotional or psychological vulnerability. Table Three highlights the significant number of women, particularly under eighteen years of age, who fit within the criteria of high levels of vulnerability.

This high level of vulnerability is illustrated by Carol:

> I left [home] with eight dollars that I took from my mother's purse. She was just going to spend it on booze anyway. I had a extra pair of pants and a shirt and a extra pair of shoes. I even forgot to bring fucking underwear, can you believe it. But I brought my small teddy bear, can you believe it.
> *Interview: Fifteen-year-old: February 6, 1989*

As revealed, the data suggest that these adolescents arrive on the streets in a very susceptible condition. These women appear to be running from less than enriching home environments. A case study of one of the respondents reveals the troubled background within the home. Jenifer, the fifteen-year-old in this case study, was the recipient of a dysfunctional home environment. The case study is as follows:

> The family first came to the attention of the child-care authorities in 1979. Jenifer lived with her mother and three brothers. Her father lived in Nova Scotia. The family was brought to the attention of the youth agencies when the eleven-year-old brother was caught shoplifting. There was a history of neglect and a tendency for the mother to use physical abuse to maintain control of the kids. As the sons grew older, physical abuse was directed at the mother by all three boys. All of the boys were involved in numerous delinquent activities. Disclosure would later indicate that the boys were physically and sexually abusing Jenifer with the mother being knowledgeable and yet not responding to the daughter's plight. Jenifer was brought to the attention of the child-care agencies because she was not attending school and subsequently because she was running away from home.

> When Jenifer was thirteen years of age, she was found in an intoxicated and drugged condition during a drug raid by police. The mother refused to allow Jenifer to come back home. Jenifer was sent to Nova Scotia for a brief period to live with her father. Jenifer was sexually assaulted by her father's friend. Jenifer ran from her father's place and he refused to take her back. Jenifer ran to Toronto where she met a pimp. Jenifer was sexually assaulted by the pimp and then procured into prostitution.

It is important to point out here that ninety percent of the respondents of this study under eighteen years of age were living away from their families because of various levels of family breakdown. Most were in the care of child-care agencies and others were living with friends. An unpublished report prepared by the Hospital for Sick Children, entitled "Sexually Transmitted Infections In Adolescent Prostitutes In Toronto" (1989: 1), highlights findings of dysfunctional characteristics:

> Most adolescent prostitutes are runaways, though not all runaways become prostitutes. These young people have often escaped from a variety of adverse circumstances including

physical and sexual abuse, incest, parental alcoholism and violence, sexual intercourse at an early age with few or no meaningful relationships, negative sexual labelling among peers.... This young, unskilled population turns to "the street" as their new home with its attraction of a socially accepting peer group, easy access to drugs and a variety of activities which may be perceived as exciting and often illicit. Drug dealing and prostitution then become the means to finance this lifestyle.

Further analysis of the family background is needed to fully understand the consequences of the characteristics of dysfunctional family experiences.

Family Characteristics

The family background or status of the 194 subjects, when they first emerged into street prostitution was such that 110 came from single-parent families. The remaining eighty-four respondents came from two-parent families. Although this distribution may appear to be somewhat equal, if one assumes that two-parent families are still the majority, then there is indeed an overrepresentation of prostitutes from single-parent families. One may wish to take this analysis further to explore the economic, social and cultural implications of single-parent families to fully understand the many problematic features that the participants may face within such family structures.

Most students of sociology will likely be exceedingly aware of the effects and implications of poverty on the family and on the individual participant. The consequences and implications of social stratification can be devastating when applied to family life. The characteristics of poverty are such that many single families do experience economic difficulties. The Statistical Abstract of the United States (1993) reports that the 1991 median household income of a two-parent family with children was $41,075.00 and the median for a female-headed family with children was $9,413.00. Moreover, the abstract reports that twenty-three percent of all preschool children in the United States are living in poverty. Similar levels of poverty can be found in Canada.

Many families, especially single-parent households headed by women, do not have enough money for the "well-being" of their members. Nett (1988: 62) notes that the well-being of the family is directly connected to financial condition and status in establishing relations inside and outside the family component:

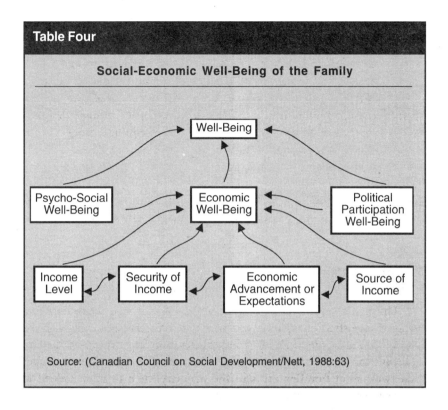

Table Four

Social-Economic Well-Being of the Family

Well-Being

Psycho-Social Well-Being

Economic Well-Being

Political Participation Well-Being

Income Level

Security of Income

Economic Advancement or Expectations

Source of Income

Source: (Canadian Council on Social Development/Nett, 1988:63)

The overall well-being of families (and of people who live alone) is highly, although surely not solely, dependent upon their economic well-being. The family and individual sense of belonging, worth, and pride—psycho-social well-being— is also an important, closely related factor. Having to live on welfare or other types of social assistance can be a degrading experience for families.... Demoralization often sets in when, because of a lack of financial resources, families feel they have no control over their housing situation, neighbourhood activities, or events in the wider political arena.

Economic well-being of the family and the individual is further illustrated in Table Four as it is expressed in a multidimensional format (Nett, 1988:62).

The family structure and function are not only influenced and articulated by economic circumstances and well-being, but financial status becomes the essential element in which families relate both within and outside social institutions. The characteristics of poverty are such that families and individuals who experience economic deprivation will be further victimized by internal and external stressors to generate dysfunctional considerations. Although economic considerations are not the only factors to influence and produce dysfunctional characteristics within the family, they are a significant factor and stressor to healthy and nurturing family life.

Beverley McKeddie, director of a youth intervention services program in Toronto, highlights the many different circumstances that have significance in developing positive and negative family characteristics. Again, keep in mind that the dysfunctional characteristics of the family force children to run to the streets. During an interview with Ms McKeddie on March 17, 1994, she reported that all of the families that come to the attention of her agency are suffering from dysfunctional behaviourial reactions that are generated by many factors including economic crisis. However, the expression of dysfunctional family relations is depicted by the individual trauma being played out by the children. This individual trauma is the result of experiences of sexual, physical, psychological and verbal abuse and neglect that the child has endured within the family structure.

McKeddie reports that many of these dysfunctional characteristics are expressed as covert abuse in that less than adequate parenting skills are fostered, which results in neglecting the needs of the children within the family unit and, therefore, the family structure and component do not meet the children's needs. Moreover, for many of these children, running from the family unit becomes a coping skill. McKeddie describes the characteristics of these children who run from their homes. These characteristics include: low to no self-esteem; self-delusions; poor physical hygiene; very little understanding of right and wrong; and no boundaries to behaviour.

McKeddie describes these children as needy kids in severe need of nurturing. The betrayal of family trust experienced by these children serves to generate individual trauma, which results in internalized trauma for the young person. McKeddie submits that this internalized trauma leaves children extremely vulnerable. These children will experience a continuum of abuse at home and on the street because of this enhanced level of vulnerability. She suggests that there are, indeed, many problematic features of single-parent families; however, she points out that two dysfunctional parents are just as destructive as one dysfunctional, maladjusted parent. McKeddie concludes by suggesting that most children have living mothers and fathers but few have "parents." She views her institutional role as "providing parental duties." McKeddie says, "that's

Table Five

Family Relationships

	No.	%
Respondents removed from home by child-care authorities	63	33%
Respondents can live at home but do not want to	25	13%
Respondents cannot return home	46	24%
Return home intermittently	41	21%
Difficulties living at home	11	6%
Reported good relations at home	8	4%
Total:	194	100%

what I get paid to do [parenting]... kids have a right to effective and nurturing parenting."

The family relationships described by the respondents were indeed less than functional. Dysfunctional aspects of family life reveal that, for most, positive family relationships were not possible because of the deteriorating family conditions. Table Five highlights the family relationships as disclosed by the respondents. The majority of the respondents emphasized the detrimental family relationship that was experienced and the feeling of urgency to remove themselves from this oppressive, painful and destructive environment.

History of Sexual, Physical and Psychological Abuse

Sexual, physical and psychological abuse at home is another area that needs to be examined to fully understand the environment. Obviously, this type of abuse would affect the nature of the family relationship, not to mention the victim's self-esteem and feelings of acceptance and rejection. Table Six provides a breakdown of the incidence of sexual, physical and psychological abuse

Table Six

Incidence of Sexual, Physical or Psychological Abuse

	No.	%
Physical abuse	70	36%
Sexual abuse	39	20%
Psychological abuse	41	21%
All three	32	16%
Total abuse reported	182	94%
Neither type of abuse reported	12	6%
Total number of respondents	194	100%

reported by the respondents. Although much debate continues as to the causality of such abuse and the incidence of adolescent prostitution, the data clearly show a high incidence of abuse among the respondents.

Bagley and Young (1987:5) disclose similar correlations:

> The present study indicates 73 percent of prostitutes were sexually abused in childhood, compared to 29 percent of a control group obtained in a random population survey. Comparison with control subjects indicated severity of sexual abuse in childhood was a significant contributor to the currently poor health and diminished self-esteem of the former prostitutes.

If nothing else the data disclose that physical, sexual and psychological abuse force adolescents from their homes and onto the street where prostitution may be one of several methods of street survival.

Education

One of the obvious implications of this extraneous home life is the diminishing of scholastic abilities, opportunities and educational focus of the respondents. The majority of the respondents did not proceed past Grade Nine. The Toronto Street Youth Project Interim Report (1986:23) cited similar findings:

> Most of the youths have a history of truancy... many of the youths are significantly behind age expectations in academic ability and, as a result of "social promotions," grades last attended may not reflect actual skill level... since these youths were on the run from home or placement... actual [school] attendance would likely be sporadic.

Only sixteen of the 194 respondents had advanced beyond Grade Ten and only two finished Grade Twelve. The lifelong implications of this formal educational deficiency and subsequent illiteracy among the respondents portray a life with very few employment and social opportunities. Assuming that the lack of education and subsequent high illiteracy levels have some impact on employment and earnings, a life of poverty can be forecast for many of these youths. If the crime traps are poverty and illiteracy, these respondents are indeed condemned to a life of despair and disillusionment.

Age

As indicated in Table One, the ages range from twelve years of age to eighteen years of age. The mean age of this sample size is fourteen-and-one-half years of age. The data again point out that many of these young women are certainly within a "vulnerable" age grouping, with very few legitimate employment and survival options. Some child-care agencies have reported apprehending children as young as ten years of age who were involved in prostitution. Fortunately, the number of children involved in prostitution at this age appears to be minimal. Most of the juvenile prostitutes are older adolescents and much smaller numbers are under thirteen years of age.

Socioeconomic Status

Juvenile prostitutes appear to come from all levels of socioeconomic status. The data certainly challenge any preconceived notions that these children are coming only from working-class, underprivileged families. The data collected from the respondents suggest that the majority grew up within a middle-class family base. Although, the data suggest that deteriorating family conditions, such as divorce and, hence, single-parent families, certainly changed the socioeconomic conditions for the parent and the children. Silbert (1980:78) reports that over two-thirds of her sample size of 200 prostitutes are from families with average or higher incomes. James (1980:21) also reports a sample size that indicated average or above average income levels. Much more research needs to be undertaken in this area. Many problematic features exist with this type of data collection as many of the respondents may have over or underreported family incomes. Many of the respondents were not privy to this type of information.

Physical and Mental Health

A study conducted at the Hospital for Sick Children, entitled *Sexually Transmitted Infections in Adolescent Prostitutes in Toronto* (1989:1), reveals some alarming findings regarding the general health, pregnancies and incidence of sexually transmitted diseases of women involved in prostitution:

> In summary, studies on fifty such youths [adolescent prostitutes] to date show that the rate of isolation of Neisseria gonorrhoea and Chlamydia trachomatous were fifty percent and forty percent, respectively, which is statistically and clinically significantly different from that of the usual population attending the adolescent medicine clinic at the hospital, in whom the rates are between four and five percent for N. gonorrhoea and eighteen percent for C. trachomatous.

The respondents interviewed for this study report similar incidents and contacts with various sexually transmitted diseases after getting involved in prostitution. Eighty-three percent of the respondents reported having contracted some form of sexually transmitted disease during their involvement in prostitution. Ninety-six percent reported that they had not contracted sexually transmitted diseases before their involvement in prostitution.

Sexually transmitted diseases, although they affect significant numbers of juvenile prostitutes, are not the only threat to this vulnerable group. The lifestyle generates experiences in the street environment that have many other negative conditions affecting the physical and mental health of its participants. McCullough (1990:30) reports that:

> Street youth chronically suffer from poor health due to exposure to the elements, poor nutrition, inadequate sleep, poor hygiene, stress and lack of preventative medical care, treatment and follow-up... females [prostitutes] may not wear sufficient clothing because it would distract 'tricks' who often identify prostitutes by their 'provocative' garb... poor nutrition often is the result of lack of money to buy nutritious meals... inadequate and erratic sleep patterns are common... life on the street begins to 'come alive' late in the afternoon and continue late into the night... stress, depression and anxiety... play a role in lowering their abilities to fight sickness.

The mental health of most of these adolescent prostitutes can be best described as in a "state of crisis." These displaced individuals are in exile from their dysfunctional family environments and bring with them a history of abuse, neglect and stress-related psychosis. Many of the respondents certainly exhibited several characteristics of their destructive family history such as violent aggressive behaviour, suicidal tendencies, lack of trust in others, depression, little or no self-respect or self-esteem, self-disillusion and limited concepts of right and wrong. The expression of this abusive background is illustrated in Table Seven, which reveals the institutional files of fifteen respondents who were in care and received diagnosis.

These files reveal many expressions of different mental health problems. McCullough (1990:35) also discloses that:

> The childhood histories of street youth are characteristically marred with physical and sexual abuse, family disfunction, and parental rejection... these youth use denial and other forms of escape... to repress or dull their underlining feelings... removes them from childhood abusive histories but they carry the unresolved baggage of abuse. The abuse and the feelings associated with abuse are perpetuated in the violence of street life.... Street youth report high levels of poor self-esteem, self-worth and feelings of powerlessness. This is evident by the high incidence of self-mutilation... and attempted suicide.

Table Seven

Youth	Age at Admission to...	Time Involved with Street	Family Status at First Admission	Presenting Mental Health Problem
Gail	15.1	2 mths	parents don't want at home	history of physical abuse by brothers physically aggressive to peers difficulty trusting others
Laura	14.10	1-4 wks	living in parental home	history of depression and possible suicide attempts severe mood swings unpredictable behaviour with violent outbreaks
Leigh-Ann	14.7	2-3 mths	removed from home by CAS	aggression towards peers erratic mood swings
Priscilla	11.8	over 1 yr	living in parental home	very volatile behaviour with episodes of severe agitation unsocialized
Tracey	14.11	1-2 yrs	removed from home at mother's request	no indication in file of behaviour suggesting a mental health problem

(continued)

Youth	Age at Admission to...	Time Involved with Street	Family Status at First Admission	Presenting Mental Health Problem
Billie Lynn	14.0	over 2 yrs	removed from home by CAS	depression highly demanding and manipulative
Kristy	15.7	6 mths-1 yr	could live at home but refuses to	mother/child conflict relates on only a superficial level
Tracy	15.5	5 wks-6 mths	parents don't want at home	physical aggression openly propositions any male no awareness of danger of lifestyle
Ann-Marie	13.5	over 2 yrs	removed from home by CAS	very withdrawn extreme mood swings highly anxious
Laura	15.0	1-2 yrs	living in parental home	highly manipulative
Marilyn	15.5	1-2 yrs	removed from home by CAS	very volatile much inner hurt and anger
Melody	15.6	no data	parents do not want at home	violent towards others minimal under-standing of the values or expectations of society

(continued)

Youth	Age at Admission to...	Time Involved with Street	Family Status at First Admission	Presenting Mental Health Problem
Sabrina	14.6	6-12 mths	removed from home at parental request	unpredictable violent behaviour
Sally	14.7	1-6 mths	removed from home at parental request	depressed and one known previous suicide attempt hysterical emotional outbursts difficulty maintaining a train of thought
Tanya	15.6	1-6 mths	parents do not want at home	severe mood swings bed-wetting (seen as stress-related)

Race

The majority of the research subjects interviewed for this effort were caucasian. The juveniles came from various racial groups, but 147 of the 194 interviewed were white. See Table Eight for a complete breakdown of race.

Other studies have found similar racial representation, such as Harlow's (1981:45) sample of 80 percent white; Silbert's (1980:37) sample of 69 percent white; James (1980:82) 61.8 percent; while Enables (1978:133) sample reported 80 percent white. Blacks were the second largest racial group represented in this sample with 20 percent, while native or indigenous culture representation

Table Eight			
Subjects	Caucasian	Black	Indigenous (Native)
194	147	39	8
	76 %	20 %	4 %

was calculated at 4 percent. Enables (1978) reported 12.1 percent black, James (1980) depicted 25 percent black, and Silbert (1980) disclosed 18 percent black. This study and the various studies available report some similarities and differences in racial background. Of course, these differences are most likely the result of the various geographic population bases in which the studies were conducted. Regardless, street prostitution crosses all racial boundaries. However, when a comparison with demographics of the general population is conducted, it is revealed that there is an overrepresentation of people representing minority groups within this prostitution category. This overrepresentation of minority groups can be correlated to social-economic status in that, again, it is observed that there is an overrepresentation of minority and marginalized group members experiencing economic deprivation. As indicated earlier, social-economic well-being and status do have significant impact on family life, family characteristics, family relations and family well-being. Therefore, the overrepresentation of minority groups within this prostitution category can be linked to the overrepresentation of marginalized groups within the poverty class in Canada and the United States.

Drug Usage

Drug usage was another area on which respondents were questioned. The majority of the subjects reported marginal use of drugs before their involvement in prostitution. The definition of "drugs" utilized within this sample was alcohol and illegal substances. One hundred sixty-seven of the 194 interviewed reported using alcohol before becoming involved in prostitution. Seventy-six of the 194 reported using illegal narcotics or designer drugs before their immersion into street prostitution.

Most of the respondents reported a significant increase in their use of alcohol and other drugs while they were being "turned out" and a continuum of substance abuse while working on the street. Although the degree of drug usage varied slightly, the data clearly demonstrate a substantial increase in the availability and use of intoxicants as part of this subculture. The portrayal of drugs as a significant expression of status and inducement is disclosed by Tracy:

> It was amazing, when I first met Cecil [to be her pimp], he took me to some clubs and he could get anything there. He kept offering me coke [cocaine] and I didn't take it the first couple of times. I just kept drinking champagne. I couldn't believe all the champagne that he bought for me. Anyway I eventually tried the coke and man did I get wiped. I think I stayed blasted for a couple of days. I just remember waking up in a hotel room with Cecil a few days later. After that I would do coke anytime I could. Cecil always had some with him. We were just partying big time. I did take some other shit, I think it was Acid or PCP or something. All I know I went crazy on that shit. That stuff is not for me.
>
> *Interview: Fourteen-year-old: July 12, 1989*

It is apparent that drug posturing and usage are all part of this street subculture. Drugs appear to be used by pimps to raise their street status or to lower the inhibitions of the women that they are trying to procure. Drugs are certainly used to emanate and enhance the "every night is a Saturday night" image and environment that plays a significant role in bonding the recruit to her new-found friends and securing her participation in this street subculture. The importance of this bonding process and the role that drugs play will be further explored and exposed in Chapter Four.

Concluding Typology

In concluding this social typology of adolescent prostitutes many characteristics can be categorized. 1) These young people are not running to the street but are running from acute crisis circumstances and experiences in their home environment. 2) These children and adolescents arrive on the street in an extremely physically and psychologically vulnerable condition. 3) The dysfunctional aspects of their family life varied, but the issue of the inability to co-habitat with family members was prevalent. 4) Significant numbers came from single-parent households. 5) Most reported some level of either sexual, physical or psychological abuse at home, and some reported all three levels of abuse. 6) The obvious ramifications of these dysfunctional family settings are the diminished scholastic accomplishments of the adolescents; most did not proceed past the ninth grade. 7) Adolescent prostitutes represent all ages with a mean age of fourteen-and-one-half. 8) Exploration of socioeconomic status suggests that adolescent prostitutes represent various levels of income groups. However, significant evidence suggests that there is indeed an overrepresentation of adolescents from the impoverished and working-class economic groups. 9) The physical and mental health of these adolescent prostitutes can only be described as extremely desperate, vulnerable, volatile and self-destructive. 10) Although the majority of the adolescent prostitutes were Caucasian, an overrepresentation of blacks and indigenous people is reported involved in this environment. 11) Drugs and other intoxicants play a significant role in this street subculture and are one of the instrumental factors that facilitate the immersion of these vulnerable groups into prostitution.

The social typology presented here is disturbing and disconcerting to those who value the lives of our young people. A significant number of our children are living a life that most of us will never experience. This typology was designed to expose the reader to some of the realities of this street subculture and how we as a society permit our children and adolescents to be exploited, violated, abused and degraded within and outside the family, in the home and on the street. The cycle of violence and exploitation that these adolescents experience is beyond acceptance in any society that claims any sense of humanity, justice or dignity. An understanding of the fragility of these adolescents is necessary to fully comprehend how these individuals are subject to predations by the sex trade managers who can readily spot these ripe candidates—ripe for immersion into a street subculture of escalating abuse and torment.

CHAPTER 4

Procurement:
The Pimp's Game

In this chapter the characteristics of the seduction method of procurement utilized by pimps are highlighted. The self-reports reveal two very distinctive methods that pimps employ to procure young women into prostitution. The seduction method of procurement is outlined to provide a greater understanding of this most effective strategy. The second distinctive method of procurement is labelled "stratagem" and is exposed in Chapter Five to reveal the methods undertaken by pimps to invoke their mandate. The characteristics and tactics of the deployment of the seduction method of procurement are exposed within this chapter to facilitate further analysis and understanding of the social site of adolescent prostitution. Moreover, this examination provides a critical analysis of the role that pimps play in the recruitment of prostitutes. This analysis reveals how this role is extended to promote and regenerate street prostitution.

The data and self-reports reveal that women who had no previous prostitution-related experiences did not run to urban centres with the intention of becoming involved in prostitution. They become involved in prostitution after arriving in urban areas in Canada and the United States. They are being procured directly or indirectly into this lifestyle by pimps. The self-reports disclose that pimps play an instrumental role in the recruit's procurement into prostitution. As suggested, there are two distinctly different methods of procurement that pimps utilize. It is asserted within this research that pimps vary their methods of procurement after giving consideration to such contingencies as age and level of vulnerability. Table Nine illustrates that the data from the self-reports represent common modes in which the subjects eventually found their way to working as prostitutes. It is asserted here that pimps who discover a woman in highly vulnerable circumstances will utilize the

Table Nine

Subjects under 18 years of age = 160

Procured by Pimp		Level of Vulnerability		Method of Procurement		
Directly	Indirectly	High	Low	Abduction	Seduction	Strategem
142	18	140	20	0	132	28
89 %	11 %	86 %	13 %	0 %	83 %	16 %

Subjects 18 years of age and older = 34

Procured by Pimp		Level of Vulnerability		Method of Procurement		
Directly	Indirectly	High	Low	Abduction	Seduction	Strategem
29	5	12	22	1	6	27
85 %	15 %	35 %	65 %	3 %	18 %	79 %

Subject Total = 194

seduction method of procurement. Pimps upon discovering women who appear to be in control of their environment employ the stratagem method of procurement.

This finding may be somewhat surprising to some observers of social exchange, as these methods of procurement are contrary to the preconceived image of how pimps operate. The societal image represented through media and popular literature conventionally depicts the pimp as using physical, coercive means to compel women into prostitution. These portrayals often suggest that women are abducted from the street and are subsequently administered various addictive drugs to compel their dependency to prostitution and to their pimp. The data reflect that this method of procurement is not utilized, but, instead, pimps employ methods of seduction and/or stratagem and not abduction. Closer analysis of the self-reports is offered here to further understand how pimps orchestrate their complex system of procurement.

Seduction Method of Procurement

The method of procurement by "seduction" that the self-reports disclose suggests that an extremely compounded projection of events is applied by pimps to seduce women into prostitution. Pimps seduce women into prostitution by strategically displaying various levels of affection, attraction and concern. These elements of emotional support bond women to pimps, and, subsequently, the women to prostitution.

The self-reports describe pimps as usually making the initial contact by way of general conversation about the need for cigarettes or inquiries as to the woman's presence in town. Early in this conversation, the pimps will ask if she is "live" or if she has a "man." This appears to be the pimps method of determining whether or not women are working as prostitutes or know the prostitution game. Within this subculture, to be "live" is to be working as a prostitute, and "square" indicates not working as a prostitute. The connotations given to this terminology, within this subculture, suggest that it is the norm in this lifestyle to be "live" and certainly not acceptable, if not deviant, to be "square." This strategy being played out is represented in the comments made by Cindy:

> He just came up to me and said, "You live or memorex?" I said, "What are you talking about?" He never did answer, but he took me out to a couple of clubs that night. He began looking after me, actually, he wouldn't let me out of his sight.
> *Interview: Fifteen-year-old: July 9, 1991*

Jenny, who had been working as a prostitute for five years, reported similar tactics utilized by pimps:

> Yea, I remember back when I started. I started with Malcom [her first pimp]. He introduced himself and he was real cool, or he thought he was. He gave me, "Are you live shit?" They all do, it's part of their little game. Man, he could read me like a book. He knew I was desperate, I didn't have a pot to piss in. I think I had only been in the city two days when I met him. He turned me out fast, but he usually looked after me. Hell, he gave me a place to stay, something to eat and clothes to wear. Man, did we used to party hard.
> *Interview: Eighteen-year-old: June 10, 1989*

If the women do not understand the pimp's question about being "live" or having a "man," the pimp then begins the process of acquiring the woman to work for him as a prostitute.

Most of the reports suggest that women are directly contacted by pimps; however, a few reports disclose that some women are indirectly contacted by pimps through other prostitutes. This is accomplished when a prostitute makes the initial contact with the perspective candidate and, subsequently, befriends her and then introduces her to the pimp. In these instances, prostitutes appear to be acting as agents for pimps. Weisberg (1985) also discovered that some of the women in her research had been indirectly contacted by pimps. She suggests that pimps might use other women recruiters for a variety of reasons. Weisberg (1985:37) notes:

> This indirect method of recruitment is more safe (in terms of avoiding legal sanctions). Second, the pimp can thus save himself considerable time. Third, he can depend on an experienced prostitute to recruit girls who have the necessary qualifications for prostitution. Fourth, experienced prostitutes are often more effective than the pimp could be, especially in recruiting young girls. Finally, the promise of friendship and companionship with other girls, more than romantic interest in a pimp, often makes joining a pimp's "stable" attractive to some recruits.

This indirect method of procurement does not appear to be employed too often; however, it seems to be an effective method of contacting potential candidates.

It is clear in the self-reports that pimps encourage and motivate their prostitutes to contact prospective candidates. Prostitutes who are able to befriend and introduce new candidates to their pimp seem to enhance their status with their pimp. Prostitutes may receive rewards of attention or nights away from working as prostitutes if they discover such lucrative investments as "new girls." Sabrina highlights her role in contacting potential recruits for her pimp:

> Yea, I was his main lady or wife-in-law, and I spent most of my time looking for new girls for Jason. Because he was older, he didn't get along well with the young kids. He couldn't compete with all the young bucks showing their magic. I would usually introduce the girls to Jason after I'd talk with them for a few hours. I had to get their trust. I would tell them

he will look after us and he would work the rest. Jason was always so proud of me when I brought another one back to the motel.

Interview: Eighteen-year-old: June 14, 1991

Kenny, a pimp who reported having six women working for him during the summer of 1988, commented:

I get the bitches to do that stuff [recruit women] I don't have time for it. You got to motivate them, it's further investment. The bitches can relate to bitches better, you know what I mean. I mean you can't let them get too close, but you've got to utilize their worth. I call it my "Bonus Point Plan." They bring me another girl, I will give them what they want, my time and more of my time. They want me so I give them me.

Interview: Twenty-one-year-old: October 17, 1988

The incentives and rewards are certainly great for prostitutes who are committed and diligent enough to increase the number of workers in the "family."

Vulnerability and Gender Relations

During this initial contact with the pimp the candidate is asked several questions about her present circumstances. Pimps ask about her current situation such as age, location of residence, closest family, how long in the city, etc. This allows the pimp to make a quick assessment of her vulnerability, then choose the appropriate method of procurement. The attraction of pimps to this vulnerable segment of society is documented in many other research efforts. Weisberg (1985:37) suggests:

Runaway episodes begin impulsively, the runaways seldom bring money with them and will frequently find themselves without resources of food and shelter...they might find shelter with strangers, but such aid might well be conditional such as an exchange of services involving drug dealing or prostitution.... Many such youths are easy marks for pimps.

Mitchell and Smith (1984:109) submit:

> The female becomes vulnerable to the pimp who offers food,
> shelter, clothing and discipline, which is usually interpreted
> as genuine caring through the provision of structure and
> control. The youth is visible on the street and is either
> approached directly by a pimp or introduced through other
> people... the youth has a high need for dependency which
> the pimp satisfies.

Shultz (1978:89) interviewed a pimp who stated, "They come to... just looking
for a pimp like me. They're practically wearing a help wanted sign."

Observations in the field in August, 1989 reveal the attraction of pimps to
these vulnerable women. Field observations were conducted at a common
location within a large shopping centre where many youth gather on a regular
basis. Young women had congregated in this area, some with knapsacks, others
walking around in much bewilderment. These obvious indicators of newly arrived,
vulnerable women were closely observed by young men, many who were
involved in pimping activities. These pimps could be observed making their
initial contact with these prospective candidates. The observations exhibited
the ease in which the young candidates could be identified, selected and then
recruited by pimps. The gross number of pimps operating on this particular
day of observations gave the feeling of vultures swarming around looking for
their next victim.

Vulnerable women are more desirable to pimps for several reasons: they
are not in control of their lives (runaways, problems at home); no means of
support (no food or money); unfamiliar environment (new to city); no social
agencies to turn to for support (on the run, under-sixteen-year-olds are often
not allowed to stay in hostels); and they are easier to exercise control over and
influence. Pimps seek out the weak and vulnerable, which are, as the data
present, all too often younger women. Mark, a twenty-six-year-old pimp, testified
that the twelve-year-old that he had procured "was an investment." He stated
that because of her tender age and vulnerability he was able to have her work
extremely long hours as a prostitute and, subsequently, he was rewarded
financially. Mark viewed this vulnerability as an asset and assisted with the
procurement process and the exercising of control over her for financial gain.
Another pimp, Junior, discloses the advantages of procuring younger women:

> You can get the younger females to be more committed to
> the cause. Man they'll work for you day and night because

they are "in love." I mean they require more work in that you got to watch them more and spend more time with them, but you can do okay.

Interview: Eighteen-year-old pimp: June 14, 1987

Pimps utilize the level of vulnerability in seducing candidates into prostitution. The self-reports reveal that pimps immediately provide cigarettes, food, emotional support and attention and describe the dangers of being young and alone on the street. Many of the young women describe this concern offered by pimps as overwhelming and depict the simple purchase of a hamburger by pimps as having monumental impact on their budding relationship. The relationship instantly takes on the characteristics of a boyfriend-girlfriend relationship, with the pimp subsequently offering to provide lodging for the woman at various hotels or with friends or family. Terry reported that:

Like a fool I fell madly in love with Dane. I just couldn't help myself. He was just so, attentive to my every need and fear. He was so comforting. I guess he was my first love.

Interview: Fifteen-year-old: June 10, 1991

The self-reports also indicate that a pimp usually becomes involved sexually with the woman within the first days of their convergence, thus bonding their germinating love relationship. Observations in the field display this flourishing love relationship in that newly arrived prostitutes are seen demonstrating obvious signs of affection for their pimp, while the pimps exhibit what appears to be care and attention for them.

Mark describes the early stage of procurement by seduction, "Pimps tell the girls that they love them because that what girls want to hear." He further explains that if a pimp shows any type of affection, she will do anything for him. The prostitutes that worked for Mark gave evidence at his trial and described this power of affection and attraction that he and other pimps are able to hold over women. A pimp named Stewart reported:

Yea, you got to be cool. You got to make them think that you love them. They don't take that much work. You got to be gentle and cool. You got to love em.

Interview: Twenty-year-old: July 13, 1991

Another pimp, Andrew, also proclaimed his strategy to manipulate younger women:

You just give them what they want. They want company. They
want someone to look after them and pamper them a bit. They
want some loving, that's all. You give them some loving and
they will do anything you want them to do.

Interview: Nineteen-year-old: July 21, 1991

Lisa, who had worked for three years as a prostitute, reported the following:

There is little doubt about it, I was really needy at the time. I
had just broken up with my first boyfriend and was looking
for someone to take his place. I'd just been kicked out of home
and I was very lonely and didn't know what to do or were to
turn. When I met Sean, he was everything. I fell madly in love
with him.

Interview: Sixteen-year-old: October 11, 1990

Pimps appear to assess the recruit's level of emotional vulnerability and to
supply her with affection and attention to fill the void. The self-reports indicate
that emotional attachment appears to have the greatest impact on the women
and that they would, indeed, do anything for their pimps.

Most of the self-reports indicate that during the candidate's early
introduction to the pimp, she did not know nor did the pimp disclose that he
was a pimp. If she discovered that her new-found friend and companion was a
pimp, often she did not terminate the relationship because the pimp did not
mention anything to her about working as a prostitute. Kathy describes her
pimp:

I figured that he cared too much for me to want me to work, I
mean he loved me. I begun to learn that he had some girls
working for him, but I figured that I was his girlfriend and the
others were his business. I guess I was a little naive about
that.

Interview: Sixteen-year-old: October 8, 1990

Jennifer also reported her experiences with her pimp as he slowly immersed her
into the prostitution environment:

Hell, I didn't know anything. I just thought he loved me. After
a couple of days I started seeing these other girls hanging

around and I started to figure it out. I knew he wouldn't hurt me or make me do anything I didn't want to do so I couldn't leave him. I would have done anything for him anyway. I guess I did, isn't that crazy.

Interview: Sixteen-year-old: January 8, 1990

The emotional attachment to pimps seems to prevent these women from recognizing that pimps may have ulterior motives.

Further Dependence — "Every Night's a Saturday Night"

The next step applied by pimps appears to be an extremely critical development in the candidate's journey into prostitution. This step immerses the candidate into the world of prostitution by exposing her to numerous prostitutes and pimps. The candidate usually receives this exposure at after hour night clubs or at various hotels. This exposure allows the new candidate to hear about the excitement of the street and the adventures associated with prostitution as described by prostitutes and pimps. This sense of excitement is further escalated for the candidate when pimps supply various drugs such as cocaine and marijuana. One young prostitute, Rebeca, describes the all night-visits and drug use at the night clubs:

Yea it was crazy, there were pimps and whores coming and going, like drugs everywhere, it was like "every night was a Saturday night."

Interview: Fourteen-year-old: November 7, 1991

A significant number of the self-reports describe this "every night was a Saturday night" concept. Exposure to these clubs and their occupants appears to have tremendous impact on the young recruit's life as she begins to bond more strongly with the pimps and to this escalated lifestyle of apparent excitement and adventure. The candidates observe women going out for the evening to work as prostitutes, and returning with the "trap" (money earned by completing acts of prostitution). These prostitutes speak of their adventures and travels of the past five hours and of the strange requests made by dates (customers). Carrie and Michelle commented on their experiences, respectively:

It was wild, Sean's girls would be getting ready to go out and it was like it was a carnival or something, everyone was excited, laughing and giggling and stuff. It seemed like fun. They would leave the hotel and I would see them later at the clubs and they were talking all about the weirdos on the stroll. We used to laugh and joke about it. I couldn't believe some of the stories, but they were true.

Interview: Fifteen-year-old: June 28, 1990

The "prep time" as they called it, was great. It was when all the hoes were getting ready. I used to help them. It was sort of exciting. It was sort of weird because you know they are going to go out and have sex. Maybe that's what made it exciting, I don't know.

Interview: Fourteen-year-old: February 17, 1989

Pimps appear to consciously expose women to a romanticized version of the "prostitution game" in an attempt to desensitize them to the realities of the sex trade.

Many of the self-reports describe these new-found friends and acquaintances as "family." It appears that the new friends become the "significant others" in the young woman's life. Sharon details her attachment to these new acquaintances:

They became my family, actually my only family. I can't call my mother family, she is such an asshole. Man we all slept together, drank together, we were going through so much. One of the hoes even helped me get out of my group home, after I got caught once. I was very loyal to them. Billy kept saying it was loyalty that would keep us together. They were the only family that I really had. They cared about me a lot. We would always look out for each other.

Interview: Fourteen-year-old: September 8, 1990

The prostitutes appear to distance any attachment to their original family and friends. Many of them began to question and sometimes disregard their previously learned values and morals. They begin to view this new lifestyle as an acceptable alternative.

Psychological Coercion —"Choosing Time"

The monetary cost of caring for and "turning out" young women is substantial. The hotel rooms, food, taxis, drugs and all the other necessary items are expensive. Pimps suggest that the women can assist their financial standing by "turning a trick." If she rejects this suggestion the pimp then suggests that she should leave or go home. Pimps tell them that they can no longer subscribe to the "family." This threat of being deprived of their pimp and a lifestyle to which they have developed a strong attraction appears to have extreme impact on what they decide to do. If she leaves, she is without her new-found special person and lifestyle. If she stays, she must work as a prostitute. These events being played out are captured in comments by Elizabeth:

> Billy said that we needed money and that he had to leave to go back to Philadelphia if he couldn't get more money. He more or less said that he couldn't afford to keep looking after me. We suddenly didn't even have enough money for food or cabs. Billy became really miserable and unhappy. He asked me to help out by turning a few tricks. I did feel somewhat obligated, I mean I needed to help out, I mean he helped me out so much. I knew he would have to leave if I didn't help. It didn't seem so bad at the time.
> *Interview: Fourteen-year-old: May 20, 1991*

A study completed by Enables (1978:209) suggests that some subjects that she interviewed reported that "they started prostitution because they were in love with the pimp and felt prostitution was necessary to maintain their relationship with him."

Pimps often subject women to a form of reverse psychology to entice them to stay and start working as prostitutes. The reports reveal that pimps often tell women that they can leave at anytime and encourage them to telephone their families. This seems to increase the desire and will to stay with the pimp. Therefore, she believes that it is her decision in "choosing" to stay and work as a prostitute for the pimp. The term "choosing" is used to describe when the women must decide if they are going to work as a prostitute or not and for which pimp. Arlene reported exercising "her choice" in staying with her new acquaintances:

> It was my choice, like he didn't force me or anything. We needed more money and he asked me to help. It was my decision. He didn't force me, I could have gone back to the home, but I didn't want to do that.
>
> *Interview: Fourteen-year-old: February 2, 1991*

Cecil, a pimp, commented on the concept of choosing:

> You can't physically force them to do it because they will just "chunk" you off. You've got to plead to their other side, their emotional side, their common sense side. They have to believe it's them helping out.
>
> *Interview: Eighteen-year-old:March 20, 1989*

Another pimp, James, reported:

> You can't do it by force, or they will get the cops involved or they will tell someone else. You got to be smooth about this. That's what this is all about. They need to believe in the "cause" or the "game." You need them committed and loyal. You've got to utilize all means necessary to get them working for you, not against you. You only get in trouble if you don't.
>
> *Interview: Twenty-one-year-old: April 7, 1988*

Weisberg (1985:12) finds that "pimps use psychological coercion to persuade young girls to become prostitutes." Shultz (1978:110) interviewed a pimp who states:

> The pimping game ain't all that physical, the whole thing is supposed to be in your mind, which is superior to a woman's. That whore should do exactly what you want her to because she should be thinking exactly the way you want her to.

The psychological manipulation engendered to provide the appearance and acceptance of choice enables the pimp to maximize his abilities in having the woman believe that she has exercised her free will in getting involved in the prostitution game. The psychological disillusionment further compounds this complex exposure and immersion and serves to compel these women into prostitution.

Reviewing the Characteristics of
the Seduction Method of Procurement:
In Conclusion

This chapter highlights the comprehensive elements of the seduction method of procurement that pimps utilize. This chapter provides the opportunity to facilitate further analysis and understanding of this social site of juvenile prostitution. Moreover, this examination provides a critical analysis of the role that pimps play in the recruitment of women to work as prostitutes. This examination reveals how this role is extended to produce and reproduce street prostitution ideology and subculture.

Pimps who discover a candidate in vulnerable conditions or circumstances utilize the seduction method of procurement. The research data that expose the characteristics of the seduction method of procurement present a reality that is somewhat contrary to the societal images and expectations as often portrayed by media. The seduction method of procurement represents a complex projection of events that are utilized to seduce vulnerable women into prostitution. Pimps seduce women into prostitution by strategically displaying various levels of affection, attraction and concern. These elements of emotional support bond the women to the pimp and, subsequently, to prostitution.

The data portray the pimp as usually making the initial direct contact with the prospective candidate to inquire as to her status. The pimp assesses her level of vulnerability and exposure to street subculture. Some reports reveal that pimps will use indirect methods of contacting potential candidates. Pimps will motivate and provide incentives to have prostitutes act as recruiters to befriend young vulnerable women.

Vulnerable women are more desirable to pimps for many reasons, but the significant factors are that they are easier to procure, influence and control. Pimps provide them with material possessions and necessities of life such as food, love, attention and support. Often, as the self-reports and field observations indicate, this relationship takes on the characteristics of a boyfriend-girlfriend exchange.

Pimps immerse young women deep into the street prostitution subculture, which serves to bond them closer to the pimp, players, prostitutes and other associates and elements of this lifestyle. The "every night's a Saturday night" concept emerges where the candidates are further induced by the fast-paced and carnival atmosphere of the time. The prostitution game is presented in a romanticized version that contributes to desensitizing the candidates to the realities of the sex trade. The young women begin to internalize the lifestyle and bond closer to their new-found acquaintances and friends. It appears that the new friends and acquaintances become the "significant others in the woman's life." The previous family ties are subjugated for these new linkages to the street.

Once she has bonded significantly to her new "family," the data reveal that pimps then begin to suggest that the candidate can assist the family by turning a trick or two. She is then given the opportunity to "choose" to stay and work as a prostitute or leave her new companions. A level of reverse psychology is employed and, in most cases, she "chooses" to stay with her new significant others.

The psychological coercion and manipulation that is exercised during this method of procurement is most successful in motivating these vulnerable recruits. The seduction method of procurement bonds the woman not only to the pimp but to a lifestyle that is presented to her as having many beneficial and rewarding components. The characteristics of the seduction method of procurement are further emphasized and exposed in the next chapter when the elements of the stratagem method of procurement are highlighted. The elements of the stratagem method of procurement provide a comparative analysis of these most effective means of producing and reproducing street prostitution.

CHAPTER 5

Strategem Method of Procurement: "Lifestyles of the Rich and Famous"

The self-reports from women who are in less vulnerable circumstances, as described earlier, suggest that the pimp's approach is very direct in illustrating that he wants them to work for him as prostitutes. This method of procurement is labelled the "stratagem method of procurement." The reports advise that pimps talk about the large amounts of money that can be earned, the glamour of travel, adventure and other grandiose images resembling the lifestyles of the rich and famous. Pimps suggest that they can develop this new lucrative, romanticized career and will provide all the support and protection that the young recruit needs. The stratagem method of procurement being played out is illustrated in comments from Beth and Karen respectively:

> He walked up to us in the club and introduced himself as "Jade." He was all decked out. He started talking about his business and we asked more about it. He said it was providing escorts for old men. He told us we could make $400.00 to $500.00 a night if we wanted to. He said he takes all his employees to Hawaii once a year as a bonus plan. He was very business about it. He even gave me his card and told me to call him if I was interested.
>
> *Interview: Eighteen-year-old: July 28, 1991*

> I was in the shopping mall and he approached me and asked if I was a model. I wasn't and he started telling me about the modelling business. He was telling me how I would make two and three thousand dollars a week with a body like mine. He

said that with his brain and my body we could make a lot of money. He said that I could purchase a new Mercedes through his company after the first year of work.

Interview: Seventeen-year-old: June 10, 1991

Women acquired by this method of procurement appear to be lured into the "prostitution game" by pimps who utilize false promises and images of grandeur.

Pimps who practice this stratagem method of procurement appear to portray themselves as managers who will accommodate the candidate's break into the sex trade business. Fitzroy, who was working as a pimp, provides some insight on the notion of sex trade managers:

Hey, I manage their affairs, I make sure they are safe. I look after them. I make sure that they feel safe. I make sure they have a good time.... I get them ready for the street and groom them so they can be successful.... You have to approach it like a business.

Interview: Twenty-six-year-old: June 11, 1988

The reports advise that a pimp gives the recruit detailed instructions of what services a pimp provides and, of course, what she is required to pay a pimp for this service, which usually works out to sixty or seventy percent of the "trap."

Women procured by this method, as those who are procured by seduction, think that it is their own rational decision to get involved in prostitution. A pimp, as with the seduction method, tells the candidate that they do nothing by force. Lori and Evelyn report this notion of "free choice" by commenting:

He outlined the game and told me what he would do for me. He told me about all the money I could make and all the wonderful places I could go. He talked about all the clothes I could buy. He then said it was my choice, I could just waste my life and be poor all my life or take control and do something for myself. He said he would be around if I chose to become involved. I ended up seeing him the next night at the club and I decided to give it a try.

Interview: Eighteen-year-old: January 18, 1991

He told me all about prostitution and what he could do for me. He did make a lot of promises and talk about all the money

I was going to make. It was a good sell, a hard sell, but when I said that I wasn't sure he said, "Think about it for a few days." He called me the next day and drove me out and around the stroll and showed me some girls who were working. It didn't seem so bad. I said yes that night, although I was wiped on coke.

Interview: Eighteen-year-old: June 1, 1990

The women believe that it is their own choice and decision to play the prostitution game, even though they are either being seduced or deceived by pimps into becoming prostitutes.

This method of procurement, as well as the seduction method, has the candidate believing that the pimp needs her and that she needs the pimp. Women who are procured by seduction believe that they and their pimp need each other for love and affection and other necessities of life. Those who are procured by the stratagem method believe that they need their pimp to protect and manage their best interests and that the pimps need them to provide an income. This notion of mutual necessity is illustrated by Debby:

I needed Leyroy to look after things. It is so crazy out there, people jacking each other up and dates beating girls. I needed him to protect me from the crazies.... Leyroy also turned me out and made sure I understood the game. I don't know what I could have done without him. Leyroy did that for me and I paid him. He needed the money and he did a good job. What's wrong with that?

Interview: Eighteen-year-old: June 7, 1991

The images of grandeur used by pimps are well illustrated by a project in 1986 in which three police officers worked in an undercover capacity and portrayed young women who had just arrived in downtown Toronto from rural Ontario, Canada. The undercover police officers were outfitted with electronic recording devices in order to record any conversation that might transpire between the officers and pimps.

The undercover police officers were positioned at various downtown locations. The appropriate surveillance was set up to ensure safety and provide observations of the movements of the officers and the pimps. When the female officers arrived downtown, the pimps were quick to notice the new arrivals. There were two separate incidence where pimps became involved in physical confrontations with each other in their attempts to get the opportunity to speak to the newly arrived prospective candidates. Several pimps scurried to speak with the three undercover officers. The pimps immediately asked the appropriate questions to determine the level of vulnerability. The pimps quickly ascertained that the undercover police officers were not entirely vulnerable and were somewhat in control of their environment. The pimps promptly articulated that they wanted them to work as prostitutes; however, these suggestions were camouflaged with images of wealth and travel to exotic places.

Pimp Dialogue: "Sitting on a Gold Mine"

The pimps used several analogies and concepts to portray and support the images of grandeur in their attempts to procure the undercover police officers into prostitution. The succeeding transcripts are a written record of some of the dialogue that pimps used in their attempt to become the sex trade managers of the undercover police officers. Jason, an established pimp, claimed:

> Some girls would sit round and just starve... know what I mean, and we mean no harm because nothing is done by force, only by common sense and logic.

> I'll put it to you like this here. What do y'all wanna do while you're here coz I won't waste your time. I won't waste your time, what do y'all wanna do while you're here. Do you want to make money. Well that's what we're here about to teach you how to make money. We're in Toronto the same way to make money.

> We have a way to making money, we have a way of making money, that makes serious money, you know what I mean, like you could make a life for yourself. Seven thousand dollars, we're talking five or six thousand a week. It would be great to have a closet full of clothes. I'm talking about buying a Rolls-Royce, drive a new car.

> First of all, it doesn't just happen like that, you have to work at it. If you have a hundred dollars for every time you had

sex, what would you say. What I'm telling you because it's you sitting here with nothing and I'm sitting here trying to offer you the world. We do it like this, we do it like this, if you found a way to make a million dollars, right, you make your million, but we will show you how to make your million. This is where my, where my conflict of interest is comin' in here. Do you know what I mean... We could sit down together and we could talk about making eight million dollars, that's only thirty thousand a piece but you individually, there's three million sitting here and you don't even know it. You're sitting on a gold mine and you don't even know it. You don't even know it. You know what I mean, cause now baby girl we can take it and we can let me tell you something about this here game, is to be sold and not told...

Alright baby, this is what you do we're talking about going to places like Las Vegas or Philadelphia or Atlantic City. Men come up because you're an attractive woman. Right. They'll say here's two hundred dollars for ten minutes of your time. You have to perform oral and have sexual intercourse with them with a condom. You do not kiss, you do not love, a love affair and that's it. You know these guys we're talking about? We're talking about the same guys you see around here and respect, doctors, judges, lawyers, presidents.... What do you think Marilyn Monroe was before she got into the movies? You every hear of Jacqueline Kennedy? I was watching Merv Griffin the other day, about three years ago, and you know who was the one they talked about as a top prize call girl before they got into show business. Jacqueline Kennedy is a call girl, that's right. Victoria Principal. I was reading in the *People's Magazine* that Margot Kidder, I mean she played that part "some kind of hero." She had to go out and play the part of a prostitute so she learned it by actors go out and do these things so they can learn how to really act like it. Right. Do you know what she said? Once she got out there, she found out that the whores, prostitutes, were articulate and very out going women. They're all out there in all new cars, wearing fur coats and doing anything and they weren't trash, as society tries to project it.

You grow up and be a like say okay to be a doctor, that's fate, you know things that you'll probably do. You want to be a doctor, you get out of school, you take twelve years of school, you take four years of college, then you take another twelve or what is it six to eight years again, your know what I mean to get your MD, your M, your MD licence, and now already you're reaching thirty, thirty-two, but now you've just begun because now you have to start on as an apprenticeship or as an intern at some other firm. But all the time who do you think is profiting off the dollars? The seven thousand in tuition that you pay and yearly books'n everything. Everyone else is makes off of you, why not you take the time out and sit there and learn how to work....

This conversation continues and the pimps make further analogies regarding parental lifestyles, the bible, travel, property, ownership and other illustrations in their attempts to glorify prostitution.

Other recorded conversations with pimps attempting to procure the undercover police officers are presented here to provide further understanding of the stratagem method of procurement. C.J., another pimp, denotes:

...you need to get yourself an apartment and some money... so when did you girls come up here... so you have to get connections now...you girls look qualified to me... you girls are qualified ladies for anything... that's right, you can if you apply now you can beat some of the students. I tell you what, I'll try tomorrow, Ill see if I can help you get into the company, it is a good escort service. Do you know what a good escort service is? It's like they phone you, right phone, not standing out there on the stroll, you know what I mean, you know what I'm talking about.... It's like, okay, you get a phone call say well listen hey, but you got to have a place. You gotta have a place with a phone. A hotel isn't really that good. So they're going to phone and take you to dinner and this and that and that and this and it's like that, right. And, you know they'll pay the bill and whatever right. You get paid for somebody to take you to dinner. Yea an escort service. That's all you have to do is sit there and have dinner with some guy.... Well sometimes they want to make deals on the side, you know, well for this and that and they pay you. Okay to just go to dinner with them, you know you get a hundred and forty dollars just to go to dinner with them and you gotta give me forty. One hundred dollars right there for you and then any other deals you wanna make on the side, right. That's totally up to you.... You can go dancing with some guy and they phone you up, usually out of town guys, businessmen. They look in the paper and they find escorts okay, they see they want to take someone to dinner, but you know whatever... and if you want you can make a deal on the side, whatever extra you know what I'm saying. Sometimes they make deals on the side so they pay you extra wages for your services. On top of the hundred, you can make whatever you make a deal for, know what I am saying.... But you gotta have a phone, you know like a hotel it isn't really that good right, you gotta have a place with a phone where they can call you.

Taped conversation: Twenty-three-year-old male:
April 23, 1986

In a conversation with C.P., another prospective pimp, the undercover police officers recorded the following dialogue:

Well let's say you get a job with my company.... I don't know what else you are going to do. Cause I know all three of you can't get a job. Most jobs doesn't pay money to you until you stay two, maybe three weeks after you get the jobs.... I'm talking about buying cars, jewellery, having your own apartment, going out, having a week's pay, having two or three hundred a day, talkin two or three thousand a week, I'm talking two or three hundred for a couple of hours. I can get people to sponsor you to give you some money, start up money.... You could make two or three hundred in one hour, well a couple of hours a night anyway. I can get you started and you can pay me back, you pay what you want to pay back when you get paid.... I want to help you out... what I'm saying right, all you girls listening or what? Okay, I'm just saying I'm going to take ya to the stroll okay, I'm telling you, I'll show you a place to go on the stroll. I'll put another girl with you that knows everything else, you know, knows what's happening. She'll go with you girls and everything right, then you will know and she will show you which hotels to go to and everything like that. What to do exactly, know what I'm saying? You know, I've already told you prices and stuff like that. You know, you'll make so much money you know, just piece me out a little bit of money for my time and stuff like that.... You girls would get two, three hundred dollars a night between all three of ya. What's that, that's six, seven, eight hundred dollars, whatever, and you know that's fast money right. That's what I'm talking about. You can make two hundred dollars a night each, at least, at least. I say two hundred dollars and that's rock bottom, two hundred dollars is rock bottom. And I'm going to give you some start up money. I gotta do all this stuff for you, know what I'm saying. I'm a nice guy right.

Taped Conversation: Twenty-year-old male: April 22, 1986

A.J., in his attempt to procure the undercover policewomen, disclosed the following information:

> ... I hate talking prices and everything else, but let me tell you what you would get for your money. I stroll, just up the road, not too far from where you'd be strolling... stroll, stroll, you know were you work right, stroll, that's what I call it, stroll.... Stroll, ya know like where you stand up, like that. Somewhere you stand up, somewhere to just, just to stand, wait, you know, stand and wait. You stand, but you girls got to know what to say... yeah, yeah, you know well, you'll be with somebody who knows right, ah you'll be with somebody who knows ya know, a good friend of mine ya know. She'll be with you, she'll show you the ropes, show you which hotels to bring the guys to whatever, some of the guys don't know which hotel to go to right. This way, twenty dollar hotel room for ten minutes.... The kinds of things you do with dates, with the guys depends.... Probably all want lays right, some of them, you know, like that.... They wear sheiks when you're doing it right, you know just do it and you know when they come, and that's it. You just ahhh whenever he comes like usually takes about two minutes right. These guys come

cause they're so horny right and that's it you've earned sixty, eighty bucks just like that and you know, you catch five dates for the night for a few hours, that's three to four hundred dollars like that, know what I mean. So you can make deals for half and halfs, whatever you want for one hundred, one hundred and twenty, one hundred and thirty bucks...

Taped Conversation: Twenty-five-year-old male:
April 20, 1986

Will commented:

> Well what I need to tell you like, I take care of you guys, okay, well you guys don't know the city too much right.... You don't know too much people. Right that's it now, listen, you can't get to know the wrong people, I can tell you don't even know who's the wrong people. Like really, you sitting here and you don't know if I'm good or bad, which I know who I am, I'm good, and I know what I'm all about, okay. Cause what I do today is gonna reflect on me tomorrow. So I try to do the best today, you know, and when I say look after you guys, I don't mean like, oh you want some, something to drink, I don't mean like that. I mean like you know, you guys need some clothes. I know the best place to get you some clothes. You know like when the hairs get done. I even know the best place to get your hair done and all that. Whatever you guys need, you know. I know where to go and get things in this city cause this is my city, you know. When I say my city, I don't own it. But, taking care of you guys is just the same thing as taking care of myself, you know. See what, it's kinda hard to put into words, you know, but once it's all happened and you know it comes around, you guys will see what I'm all about, see what I'm talking about, you know.

> Well you see I'm different, see I'm different, see I let the three of you guys go outside and you guys, between each other, probably bring in nine bills. Okay, I wouldn't touch none of that okay.... That's all for you guys to spend on yourself. Take care of yourself. Get yourself some nice clothes and all that,

you know. Okay, you gotta look good when you're out there and once you're looking good you make the money, no problem, I mean like, like this doesn't look too bad. But you know, you go out there and you see what I mean, you see all the ladies in dresses and all that, you know, like for instance when you remember when you were downstairs in Valentino's, you see how those ladies dress.... See I'm on a plan, a master plan, see if y'all, if y'all were with me now, that'd be coming from me, my expenses, and I would go look for the things you need, which is no problem. I'll do that, you know coz I know a few people around here so I could get some money from and all that.... Once you start making some money, start taking care of yourself first, yeah, that's what I'm trying to tell you... we gotta take it one step at a time, you know, one step at a time.

Taped Conversation: Eighteen-year-old male:
April 18, 1986

When one listens to the conversations on the recorded tapes, one is astonished at how convincing the pimps are in their efforts to procure these undercover policewomen. One could speculate that if these pimps ever decided to sell life insurance, they would be millionaires in a week. The convincing nature of these pimps is well illustrated in outlining the effect of this discourse on the undercover police officers. The immersion of the officers into this world of pimping had a profound effect on their personalities. Within four days of the project, the officers became aware of the impact of this immersion on their personalities. The young officers, for the most part reared in middle-class suburbs of Toronto, found that the rational and convincing arguments put forward by the pimps were very overpowering. The arguments that the pimps expressed began to challenge the officers' own personal values and beliefs. One of the officers commented on the effect of this exposure to pimps and their milieu:

It was crazy. I've worked undercover drugs and other projects but nothing affected me like this. The pimps were so convincing. They were so suave and sophisticated for the most part. It was almost like they were psychologists or something. They were playing with our heads, our minds, our conscience, our sense of right and wrong. They were trying to read us, read our minds as they went along. They would keep changing their tactics and strategies as they talked to find our weaknesses. They get right into your head and try to get you to think like them. It was almost like they were trying to **brainwash** you or something. Very dangerous people. I can tell you this much, a kid doesn't stand a chance against these guys. No way. They'll have them out on the street in a couple of days.

Conversational Interview: September 26, 1986

The effectiveness of these pimps to even remotely challenge the morals and values of police officers who had the benefit of a reasonable family life certainly illustrates the likely success rate of pimps procuring younger, vulnerable women who have not had the benefit of a substantial home environment.

Reviewing the Characteristics of the Stratagem Method of Procurement: In Conclusion

The method of operation employed in both the seduction and stratagem schemes are contrary to the societal image of pimps. The societal image often depicts pimps as abducting women for the purpose of prostitution. This misleading image appears to enhance the pimps' ability to procure young women into prostitution. The misinformation prepares women to safeguard themselves against physical attack from pimps; however, it leaves them exposed to the reality of psychological coercion and manipulation from males who choose to employ these methods of seduction and deceit. Women in the self-reports were very vulnerable to the unexpected psychological coercion and manipulation applied by pimps.

This chapter illustrates that the stratagem method of procurement is successful in convincing candidates to become involved in prostitution. The convincing arguments, the images of grandeur and the appeal to aspirations of achievement ensure that this method of procurement is most effective in its purpose. Analysis of the pimp dialogue, as related in this chapter, reveals that pimps utilize a very masterful and competent strategy to convince women that prostitution is a lucrative and rewarding vocation. Pimps espouse a discourse that speaks of large amounts of money, the glamour and circumstance of travel, and the acquisition of various material possessions and enhanced prosperity. Pimps utilizing the stratagem method of procurement provide an image of the prostitution environment that resembles "the lifestyles of the rich and famous." Whereas a critical inspection of the prostitution ambience depicts a social reflection of "the poor and the exploited." The forthcoming chapters will challenge this romanticized image of prostitution, as presented by pimps, and reveal the violence and degradation that pimps impose on those who "choose" to work as prostitutes.

CHAPTER 6

Training: Getting Started — "Turned Out" Applying the Trade

If the woman chooses to stay with the pimp and her new street friends, she "chooses" to become involved in prostitution, as the seduction method of procurement suggests. If she is convinced by the pimp's exaggerated description of prostitution, she "chooses" to be involved in prostitution, as the stratagem method of procurement demands. The next stage is a significant one in the further immersion into the prostitution environment. This chapter highlights the significant factors of "learning the game" or being "turned out." The training process will be examined to expose the job training strategies and orientation procedures that pimps employ in developing young women for prostitution. Moreover, this examination moves beyond analysis of the street rules and regulations, to reveal the "socialization processes" and the "subcultural components" that are engendered and imposed while "learning the game." The revealing of the socialization process and the subcultural components expose the strategies that pimps utilize to indoctrinate new recruits to conform without question to the rules, expectations and roles as imposed by pimps and the street environment.

The training and subsequent bonding to prostitutes, pimps and the street environment ensure adherence to the ideology represented on the street. The ideology embraced within the prostitution environment is produced and reproduced, which contributes to neutralizing the individual identity of the new recruit and weakens any attachment to previously learned values and norms. The recruit's complete immersion into this environment facilitates the internalization of the "prostitution role." This adoption and internalization of the prostitution role serves to ensure the recruit's adherence to the pimp and the street subculture

As the self-reports disclose, if a woman "chooses," it means that the pimp will need to train her to work as a prostitute. The self-reports suggest that the young women are turned out usually by pimps with assistance from their "wife-in-law." The wife-in-law is the pimp's "main lady" or the prostitute that a pimp trusts with the task of turning out a new candidate. The training consists of being apprised of all the rules of the street sex trade business. The number one rule is "don't tell the police that you have a pimp," and the number two rule is "don't hold back trap" (money). The number three rule is "don't talk to other pimps," and the number four rule is "don't talk to the police any longer than you have to." The candidate is also instructed on how to recognize plain-clothes police officers, bad dates and dangerous situations, how to perform various sex acts, condom use, the exchange of money, how much money to charge for various sex acts, how much money to make each night and other essential knowledge that they are required to know if they are to survive in this game of sex for money. Sharon reports her experiences while being turned out:

> It all seemed to happen so fast. I mean, Cecil took me out on the stroll a couple of times and we watched the girls coming and going. He kept telling me what was going on and kept giving me different circumstances and talking about what to do if it happened that way. He pointed out several undercovers and pimps. He told me how to deal with them. He stayed with me the first two nights when I broke.
>
> *Interview: Sixteen-year-old: July 18, 1990*

Mary commented on her experiences of learning the game:

> It was kinda weird. It was so exciting, I mean Kenny kept it so exciting in getting me ready. He was laughing and singing as he was showing me what to do. It was like we were rehearsing for a big show or something. Getting ready for opening night or something. Kenny and Stewart told me everything I guess. You still learn a lot once you're out there.
>
> *Interview: Fifteen-year-old: May 5, 1991*

Caplan (1984:140) suggests that pimps have developed a system of "outreach, intake, orientation, job development, on the job training, housing, peer support, role models, and incentive programs that are all part of what he offers." Pimps and their wives-in-law provide the necessary information and training to facilitate the recruit's further involvement in the prostitution environment. This immersion moves the candidate closer to the initiating ritual of "turning the first trick," to get her ready to "break" for the first time, thus securing her commitment to the sex trade.

Applying the Trade: The "First Trick"

The females are told that their pimp or one of the "players" are close by if they need anything. The females are sent out on the street with the wife-in-law to "turn her first trick." The first trick establishes her newly acquired position in the family. The self-reports describe the experience of turning the first trick as exciting, but at the same time frightening. The pimp's wife-in-law usually went with the new recruit on the "first date," in an attempt to reduce the fear that the candidate may be experiencing. Many women characterize the first date as embarrassing, but submit that it is over quickly and generates money swiftly. Marlene describes her first trick:

> It was embarrassing standing on the street, like everyone going by was looking at us because they know that we are working, but the guy drove up and we went with him. I did what I had to and made my first sixty dollars. It was easy, I guess but I never looked back, everything was happening so fast. I remember how happy and excited Kenny was when I told him that I broke. He made me feel good about all of it.
> *Interview: Fourteen-year-old: June 17, 1991*

The self-reports depict the importance of turning that first trick and the subsequent endorsement that is received from the pimp.

The significance of turning the first trick within this subculture is indeed material in its implications and consequences. The turning of the first trick further immerses the recruit deeper into the prostitution environment. This "socialization process" serves to bond her to other prostitutes and to the street subculture. This ensures adherence to the ideology represented and fostered by the pimp. Female prostitutes are "socialized" to embrace the street subculture and are therefore required to internalize the values and beliefs of the street in order to belong to the family. The cultural values and norms of the street subculture include many behaviours and beliefs that may be contrary to those expressed by the dominant culture. Heather describes this internalization of the street subculture:

> Ya, I couldn't believe how fast everything was happening and I couldn't believe the things I was doing. I mean, I was a new person, I mean I was doing things that I never would have done before. Especially some of the sex things. I started acting that part and I was proud of it. I sort of loved to see the reaction to straight people when I told them I was a 'Hoe.'
> *Interview: Sixteen-year-old:April 10, 1990*

Jamie reported:

> It's all sort of like a dream or maybe a nightmare, but I just got into it big time, like it's hard to explain. But, like when I was working, I actually seen a couple of my old school fiends downtown and they didn't even recognize me. They all said I had changed so much. I guess I was putting on a bit of a show for them. I think I scared the hell out of them when I started talking about blow jobs and lays. I really believed that I was one big-time Hoe.
> *Interview: Sixteen-year-old: March 8, 1989*

Within the street prostitution subculture, the values and norms express many behaviours that would receive much negative stigma within the dominant culture. Such activities and values as law-violating behaviour, fearlessness, daring, shrewdness, excitement, danger and freedom from external constraints of the conventional norms and values of the family, state or school are all expressions that are manifest, endorsed and encouraged within this street subculture. The prostitute is required to internalize these norms and values and therefore internalize the roles and attitudes of street prostitution. This internalizing ensures that the woman begins to see herself within the social role of "prostitute" and therefore will play out that role. The official labelling of deviant or delinquent behaviour results in the internalization of a delinquent or deviant self-image or conscience, and hence continued involvement in delinquent or deviance activities or, in this case, continued participation in prostitution.

Turning the first trick has other significance in regards to the role of pimps. Pimps appear to realize the importance of this immersion to new values and norms within this street subculture. The self-reports disclose that it becomes most evident that the prostitute's status with her pimp changes significantly after she turns the first trick. The pimp immediately imposes a "turning out fee" or "street charge," she is now financially indebted to the pimp. This significant change in status reduces the woman to property or an investment that can be redeemed or exploited for considerable financial reward. This change in status appears to affect the pimp-prostitute relationship considerably as the working relations descend to violence.

The self-reports suggest that prostitutes are usually instructed to give all the money that they earn to their pimp. Pimps prescribe the amount of money that prostitutes are to earn, which is usually five to seven hundred dollars an evening. A prostitute who is found to have held back the "trap" is subject to severe discipline. The relationship between the two becomes more strained or conflictual as the financial intentions of the compact begin to be exercised by the pimp. Brenda and Kelly report respectively:

> Ya, things changed a lot after I was turned out. Jason seemed to stop really caring for me. He was spending more time with other girls. He just kept asking for money. He started to get angry because I wasn't making enough. Sometimes I was bringing in $600.00 to $800.00 a night. He still wasn't satisfied.
> *Interview: Fifteen-year-old: July 18, 1991*

> He [her pimp] took everything. He said he would give back my share of the money at the end of the month. He said he was looking after some financial matters. I kept giving him all my money and he would give me a few bucks for food and condoms and stuff. That was about it. Once I kept some money back, I think it was one hundred dollars, and he found out. He beat me that night. He was so offended that I didn't give him all the money. You learn quick, I thought that he was going to kill me.
> *Interview: Seventeen-year-old: May 12, 1991*

The pimp's appropriation of all the money that the prostitute earns further compels reliance on the pimp. One prostitute who gave all the money she earned to her pimp describes how wonderful her pimp was because he bought her a line of cocaine each night after she finished working. She did not seem to recognize that she has just given her pimp six hundred dollars so he could purchase fifty dollars worth of cocaine for her.

Conclusion: Reviewing The Findings

The unyielding, vigilant and strategic engagement of the rules and regulations of the street sex trade permits pimps to ensure significant control over their workers. The significance and importance of "being turned out" certainly identifies the rigorous adhesion to set rules and regulations, but more pertinent is the ensuring of ideological adherence to the prostitution subculture. The ideological adherence not only serves to neutralize the stigma attached to the sex trade by the dominant culture but also facilitates the internalization of the prostitution role. The internalization of the prostitution role allows for the rejection of earlier learned values and norms and stimulates the internalization of the new values and norms present and encouraged in the prostitution environment. The woman's internalizing of the prostitution role prescribes her to think, act, walk, talk and live the foreseen "social role" of a street prostitute. She begins to see herself as labelled, living, acting and thinking as a prostitute and therefore committed to the prostitution environment and lifestyle. The "turning out" process is about learning rules and expectations of the sex trade, but more imperatively it is about adopting, adapting and internalizing the role of street prostitute.

CHAPTER 7

Working Relations:
The Descent into Violence

The relationship that the new prostitute has with her pimp continues to demonstrate the characteristics of a boyfriend-girlfriend or a manager-worker association, even though she is now working for him as a prostitute. However, it is a relationship that is full of conflict. Prostitutes often become jealous of other women that pimps have working for them. Many prostitutes are initially unaware that their pimps have several other prostitutes working for them. The self-reports indicate that many prostitutes became enraged upon this discovery. They begin to question the economic arrangement or become dissatisfied with the pimp's managerial services or guarantees of protection. They can also become physically and emotionally exhausted very quickly from participating in this excelled lifestyle and, therefore, start to question the relationship. Stacey illustrates this fatigue factor:

> He had me out there every night of the week and we were partying every night, like I was doing all the work and giving the money to him while he sat inside at the clubs talking to all the women, I finally had enough and that was when he started getting rough.
>
> *Interview: Fifteen-year-old: April 17, 1990*

Jennifer recounts similar events:

> He said that he was going to give me protection, but hell, in one week I got jacked up twice and beaten by a bad date. I ended up with eight stitches in my arm. But Evin was no where

to be found when all that shit was going down. He would always show up at the end of the night for the money. I got mad and that's when he accused me of trying to "chump him off" [leave him]. That's when he started slapping me around.

Interview: Sixteen-year-old: June 7, 1990

The reports describe the relationships as descending further into turmoil. This increase of violence suggests that the pimp is losing his ability to psychologically coerce and exercise control over the prostitute and thus begins to resort to physical violence in his attempt to continue his control. Shultz (1978) suggests that when a pimp has to resort to physical violence, he is losing respect. A pimp that Shultz (1978:110) interviewed states:

There's something wrong with your game or maybe you if you have to be physical all the time. You're either a beating freak, a natural gorilla or else you're losing control of your women.

Pimps move from psychological persuasion to strategically utilize physical coercion to keep prostitutes productive. The level of violence inflicted on prostitutes at this stage of the relationship varies. Some reports depict horrific scenes of brutality, but most disclose a variety of threats of physical violence made by pimps. The threats exert a "psychology of fear" upon the prostitutes, as pimps display weapons and openly discuss what happens to prostitutes who violate the rules. These threats, displays of weapons and assertive posturing serve to generate an environment of fear. Karen and Jackie report this environment of fear respectively:

He kept reminding us of what would happen if we fucked with him. He would always take his knife out and play around with it. We knew what he meant.

Interview: Sixteen-year-old: April 17, 1990

Keith had caught me and took me to a stairway. He pushed me backwards and I fell down about fifteen stairs. I thought for sure that I broke my leg. While I was laying in the stairwell, he brought Nancy over to show her that I was laying there in pain. He told her she was next if she tried anything stupid.

Interview: Fifteen-year-old: August 10, 1991

Amanda and Sharon, respectively, reported similar violent acts that generated much fear and compliance:

> He beat Karen in front of us with a pimp stick [coat hanger]. He then took a cigarette and put it to her breasts. He was burning her and she was screaming. You could smell her flesh burning. He just didn't give a shit. He kept saying he had to make an example out of her so he could spare us from having to be taught a lesson like her. He made it seem as if he was doing us a favour. I got the message.
>
> *Interview: Sixteen-year-old: June 23, 1987*

> Every Saturday night you would hear about someone being beaten up. That news really travelled fast on the stroll. It was usually because some Hoe didn't give all the trap or was seen talking to another pimp.
>
> *Interview: Sixteen-year-old: July 18, 1990*

Pimps utilize the publicity produced over the death of a prostitute by candidly submitting that the deceased prostitute's pimp was responsible for her death as she had violated her pimp's rules. This claim is often made, even though conclusive evidence demonstrates that the prostitute died of natural causes or was the victim of a bad date. Amy and Carol, respectively, articulate this street hysteria:

> The police said that she was killed by a bad date in a blue Ford truck, but everyone on the street said it was Dwayne. I don't think Dwayne could actually kill someone, but everyone on the street thought he did it. I don't know, but he did get more respect on the street after it.
>
> *Interview: Fifteen-year-old: June 4, 1991*

> She supposedly died of a drug overdose in the stairway. At least that's what the police said in the papers. Supposedly heroin. Her pimp was in jail so it couldn't have been him. She did testify against him about eight months before she died and everybody knew she signed on him. Most people figured it was a debt owed to her pimp. The police just said she choked on her vomit.
>
> *Interview: Seventeen-year-old: April 17, 1991*

Seduction/Strategem to Abduction

Women in the self-reports, for the most part, describe the relationship with their pimp as very satisfying and pleasant during the outset of their encounter, regardless of which method of procurement their pimp utilized. However, as described earlier, many of the women begin to question the relationship within a short period of time. With the relationship deteriorating, many prostitutes disclose that they would be subjected to physical abduction by pimps. If the woman attempts to leave her pimp or violates one of his rules, she is often subjected to being abducted from the street and physically disciplined by the pimp. Kathy and Sharon, respectively, describe being abducted and assaulted after leaving their pimp:

> I had left Jason and wanted to take a break from working so I just hid out at a couple of hotels. I was able to hide out for four days until he caught me. He actually choked me out. He beat me and I was black and blue all over. He made me work three times as hard to make up for the lost money. He watched me continuously for three weeks after that.
>
> *Interview: Fifteen-year-old: April 18, 1990*

> When I left, Keven caught me at the mall and told me to come with him or he would slit my throat right there on the spot. He took me back to the hotel and beat me. He kept saying that he had invested too much time in me to let me chump him off like that. He told me I would have to pay him $4000.00 if I wanted to leave.
>
> *Interview: Thirteen-year-old: June, 17 1987*

Pimps claim a "colour of right" over prostitutes, as they have invested time and energy in turning out. This abduction is usually described as violent and results in the woman being physically forced to continue to engage in prostitution. Table Ten illustrates this shift to abduction regardless of the method of procurement that pimps employ.

The Toronto Street Youth Project Report (1986) reveals that pimps are the most frequent physical abusers of young prostitutes under sixteen years of age. The Badgley Report (1984:118) also documents this high incidence of physical abuse inflicted on prostitutes by pimps in noting that "four in five girls who had worked for pimps had been beaten, and in some instances, seriously injured by

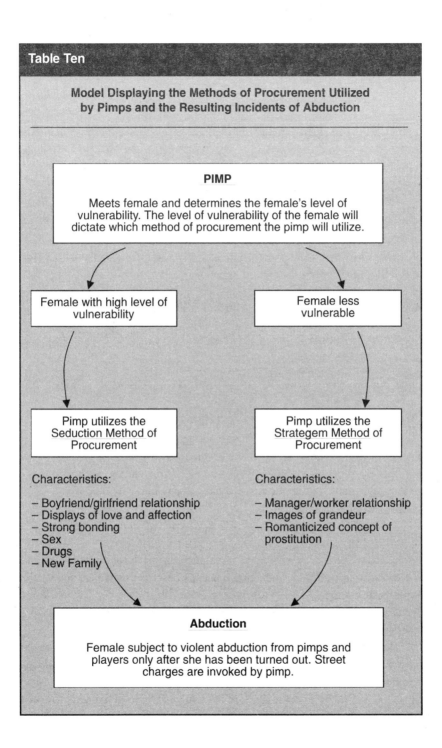

Table Ten

Model Displaying the Methods of Procurement Utilized by Pimps and the Resulting Incidents of Abduction

PIMP

Meets female and determines the female's level of vulnerability. The level of vulnerability of the female will dictate which method of procurement the pimp will utilize.

Female with high level of vulnerability

Female less vulnerable

Pimp utilizes the Seduction Method of Procurement

Pimp utilizes the Strategem Method of Procurement

Characteristics:

– Boyfriend/girlfriend relationship
– Displays of love and affection
– Strong bonding
– Sex
– Drugs
– New Family

Characteristics:

– Manager/worker relationship
– Images of grandeur
– Romanticized concept of prostitution

Abduction

Female subject to violent abduction from pimps and players only after she has been turned out. Street charges are invoked by pimp.

these men." Eight-five percent of the subjects interviewed for this effort revealed that they had been endangered by violent abductions and several physical assaults at the hands of pimps. These violent encounters were often the result of non-compliance with rules or regulations as imposed by the pimp. Many of these women were so fearful for their lives that they sought the assistance of social and law enforcement agencies in an attempt to escape the apprehension and terror.

"Street Charge"

Pimps impose a "street charge" on prostitutes, which is a "turning out" fee that pimps demand for their efforts of "qualifying" candidates to become prostitutes. The "street charge" stipulates that prostitutes must pay their pimp a sum of money, usually one to two thousand dollars, if the prostitute "chooses" to leave her pimp. A female with a street charge imposed on her is subject to abduction from any pimps or players who are aware that such a charge had been put into action. Wendy and Bridgett, respectively, report their experiences with street charges:

> I heard that he had put a $2500.00 street charge on me, so I kept hiding. About two days later this guy comes up to me that I didn't even know and grabs me. I fought all the way, he just kept twisting my arm. I thought he was going to snap it in two. This guy takes me back to Kenny and he slaps me and gives this guy my $200.00 that Kenny took from my wallet.
> *Interview: Fourteen-year old: August 15, 1990*

> I knew I was in trouble when the same guy drove past for the third time. I tried to get away but he had two other guys with him. He said that I was worth $500.00 to him. He took me back to Cecil, and sure enough he paid the guy $500.00.
> *Interview: Thirteen-year-old: June 16, 1989*

The finder of these renegade or non-compliant prostitutes, according to this street culture, is authorized to abduct females and return them to the pimp who has invoked the charge. The finder receives an honorarium for his discovery, abduction and subsequent return of the woman to her pimp. The women are usually subjected to physical assaults and are compelled to engage in acts of prostitution to pay the leaving fee and have the street charge eradicated.

Kenny, a pimp who gave evidence at his own trial, explains that when the prostitute "chooses" to go to a new pimp, the two pimps meet and discuss a reasonable street charge. When the prostitute raises enough money under the encouragement of her new pimp, she pays her original pimp. However, she does not know that the two pimps have collaborated to split the money that she has just earned. Kenny declared that "this is one of the games that we pimps play to make more money from them before she punks you off." Teddy reports:

> You know man, it's part of the game. We [pimps] look out for each other you know. We have to help each other out or the bitches will drive you crazy. It's part of the game. If she's going to leave, she's going to pay and that's the way is. Like nobody does anything for free, right. It's about lost revenue if you get what I mean. I mean you shouldn't be beating her, but you got to look after your investments.
>
> *Interview: Twenty-one-year-old:March 18, 1987*

Mark notes:

> It's sort of a way to provide incentives, you know work incentives to keep them working. Otherwise the Hoes will just stand around all night talking and stuff. I'm just getting paid for my work, it's money for services rendered.
>
> *Interview: Twenty-three-year-old: April 2, 1987*

Julie, who worked as a wife-in-law, reports:

> I was Johnny's wife-in-law for almost two years, and we likely put fifteen street charges or more on different girls during that time. It was usually the best way to get the girls to be really productive because they were usually scared by then. If you could keep track of them you could really get some fast cash. My job was usually to watch them and collect the money as soon as they broke and give it to Johnny.
>
> *Interview: Nineteen-year-old: June 14, 1989*

The street charges serve to generate a significant cash flow for pimps in payment for their time and energy in "qualifying" prostitutes. The time that the pimp invested is calculated into a monetary sum and the status of the prostitute within this environment is reduced to the level of property to be bought and sold.

Consequences of Exploitation:
The Fears and the Disclosure

The environment of fear that pimps generate and demand results in very limited disclosure by prostitutes in regards to any information about their experiences with pimps. One of the very strong messages that is emitted from the self- reports is: "Don't tell the police that you have a pimp!" This emphasis is illustrated in reports from Carol and Mary, respectively:

> He told me that if I said anything to anyone about him, he would find me and kill me. When I got picked up by the police once, he questioned me and slapped me around to see if I had told the police anything.
>
> *Interview: Seventeen-year-old: March 17, 1990*

> Keith always kept saying "don't sign on me." This meant signing a statement against him for the police. He always said if I signed on him, he would get me. When I did sign on him, he did get one of his friends to threaten me, but he got arrested too. I still keep looking over my shoulder.
>
> *Interview: Sixteen-year-old: February 10, 1989*

This rule is ardently imposed and enforced on the street by pimps and is severely imbedded within the prostitute's understanding of the street.

When prostitutes requested the assistance of social services or law enforcement agencies, they usually only wanted shelter so they would be at a safe distance from their pursuing pimp. Beverley McKeddy, program director of a group home that specializes in providing services for adolescent prostitutes, notes:

> Many of these girls come to us in fear for their lives. Most have been repeatedly beaten and threatened and only want shelter and a sanctuary from their pimp. These children usually need several weeks of constant care before they begin to disclose their experiences on the street. It is only after these children believe that they can trust the staff and that they are safely away from their pimp, then and only then, they may disclose information. It is certainly on their time.
>
> *Interview: September 16, 1994*

Yaworski (1986:4) suggests:

> Although few girls initially admit to working for pimps, most
> later admit to having one or are known on the street to work
> for someone... we quickly learned that when the girls used the
> term "boyfriend," it frequently meant "pimp."

The Badgley Report (1984:119) also recognizes the reluctance of prostitutes to disclose information about pimps:

> One-third of the female juvenile prostitutes admitted that they
> were working or had previously worked with pimps. Because
> of the girls fear of these pimps, it is evident that this is a sharp
> underestimate of this practice.

After being exposed to this street subculture, the women interviewed for this study did not usually wish to give any information about their involvement with pimps during their outset of being admitted to youth centres. This reluctance to give complete or accurate information obviously creates several difficulties for child-care workers, law enforcement officials or researchers in trying to obtain valid background information. Most of the 194 prostitutes who gave the self-reports that are adopted for this study originally refused or gave only limited disclosure about their involvement with pimps. They provided more information once they believed they were safe and felt they could trust the staff of the youth centres and, subsequently, the researcher.

The women that are forthcoming about their pimps are, for the most part, those who have been admitted into various street youth projects. It appears that when they are admitted into these facilities, disclosure increases with the amount of time that they are in contact with staff and the police officers assigned to operate these projects. Staff at many of these facilities spent considerable time debriefing the women who gave self-reports for this study. The staff spent considerable time in directing them to scrutinize the relationship that they have or had with their pimp. The staff encouraged them to assess the circumstances that saw them become involved in prostitution. The women usually began to recognize the exploitive aspects of the relationship and subsequently acknowledge the need to eliminate the bond with their pimp. This acknowledgement serves to accommodate their rehabilitation process.

The staff of these facilities allowed the women to stabilize their fear of their pimps in order to facilitate the disclosure process. The women often suggested that they believed that it didn't matter where they hid because their pimps would be able to locate them. The staff spent considerable time teaching the realities of the power of the pimp. One street social worker was overheard to explain that "the biggest thing a pimp has is his mouth." The women needed to recognize that if they gave sufficient disclosure about the relationship with their pimp to warrant legal sanctions, the pimp would be incarcerated. They needed to be further advised that when their pimp was incarcerated past experience has illustrated that it is unlikely that there will be pimps or players looking to harm anyone. In reality what occurs is that other pimps and players are kept very busy attempting to recruit the incarcerated pimp's prostitute for their own use and are not concerned about who is disclosing information.

Further Consequences of Exploitation: The Cycle of Violence

In order to fully understand why a prostitute may remain with a pimp who has subjected her to various levels of violence and other forms of degradation, elements of a cycle of violence are offered. Further analysis is needed of this pimp-prostitute relationship to assess this cycle of violence model and determine how central this cycle is in forcing women into this environment.

The prostitution subculture generates and demands significant social isolation from individuals outside the "prostitution game." The social stigma and labelling process ensures that prostitutes isolate themselves within their own subculture. The prostitute, therefore, has very little access to personal support networks outside the prostitution environment. Her fears for her own safety or the safety of her loved ones often keeps her quiet. She may feel shame and embarrassment about working as a prostitute and this keeps her at a significant distance from others not involved in the prostitution game. Her social isolation limits her opportunities for realistic feedback that might modify her perceptions of her situation. Her loneliness and isolation then serves to increase her dependence on her pimp, the very person who promotes and stimulates the isolation.

Social isolation generates into a level of personal and social helplessness. The prostitute is often in a state of "learned helplessness." This means that her attempts to control her environment, escape or avoid the violence will be unsuccessful. This perceived inability to change her social circumstances brings about a sense of powerlessness that can lead to a belief that nothing she does will change the situation.

The enhanced level of personal and social helplessness condemns the woman to internalize the blame for her social circumstances. The prostitute often believes that she is to blame for the violence as she may have violated one of the pimp's rules or regulations. Pimps often tell their prostitutes, "Why do you make me hit you? If you would only do what you are told this would not happen." The prostitute may try even harder to follow the pimp's rules more closely, not realizing that the violence has little to do with her behaviour or personality.

There may be a level of ambivalence or inconsistency in the relationship that becomes problematic. The pimp may not be violent all the time. There may be periods of time when the prostitute believes that her pimp is kind and in some cases loving. This is the crux of her ambivalence. She wants the violence to end, but may not want her relationship with her pimp to end.

She may begin to internalize the oppression. When any group believes it is inferior and deserves to be treated badly, this makes it easier for the bad treatment to continue. Such beliefs are sometimes called "internalization of oppression." The prostitute may already see herself as inferior and when she is subjected to violence this act may serve to confirm her suspicion that "something is wrong with me."

The result of social isolation, learned helplessness, internalizing the blame, the ambivalence factors and the internalization of the oppression is a low self-esteem. The end result of repeated abuse and violence is a battered self-esteem. The prostitute's sense of worthiness, self-confidence, self-image, and belief in her abilities have all been damaged. Table Eleven visualizes this progression of the cycle of violence.

Conclusion:
Reviewing the Findings

The characteristics of the pimp-prostitute relationship change significantly after the prostitute has been recruited, turned out and a street charge levied against her person. The data present a disturbing litany of incidents in which this relationship descends to manifest various levels of violence inflicted on prostitutes to ensure their compliance with the social order of street prostitution. Once the pimp's ability to psychologically coerce the prostitute to continue to produce revenue has failed, the pimp moves to ensuring his will by utilizing various threats and acts of physical violence. The environment of fear that is

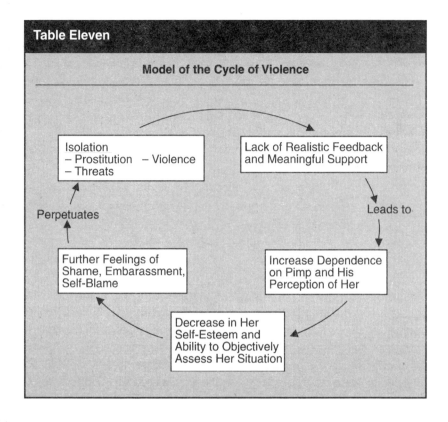

Table Eleven

Model of the Cycle of Violence

Isolation
– Prostitution – Violence
– Threats

Lack of Realistic Feedback
and Meaningful Support

Perpetuates

Leads to

Further Feelings of
Shame, Embarrassment,
Self-Blame

Increase Dependence
on Pimp and His
Perception of Her

Decrease in Her
Self-Esteem and
Ability to Objectively
Assess Her Situation

generated increases the level of dependence of the prostitute to her pimp and subsequently ensures compliance with the prostitution lifestyle.

Violence is further escalated when prostitutes attempt to leave their pimps. The pimp-prostitute relationship has evolved to a status in which the pimp has established property rights over the woman in payment for "turning her out." The prostitute as property is materialized by "street charges" being imposed on females, which subjects them to abduction and compliance. The street charge asserts that prostitutes can purchase their freedom or release themselves of their pimp's contractual obligation if they provide sufficient financial remuneration. The data suggest that the street charge process is often orchestrated and collaborated between the two pimps without the knowledge of the prostitute. This strategy is again another method in which to motivate and ensure that the pimp can redeem as much financial gain as possible.

The obvious consequences of this exploitation are manifest in the many fears, the limited disclosure and an emerging cycle of violence that often forces women into prostitution. The women running to the youth shelters for protection from their pimps are often terrorized and suffer from many distorted misgivings regarding the abilities of their pimps to locate and apprehend them. The staff of the youth centres spend a significant amount of time debriefing, stabilizing and providing support to ensure that the women feel safe and to generate their personal confidence. Only after a woman feels safe and distant from her pimp will she provide disclosure as to her experiences and her relationship with her pimp. This exploitation generates an environment of fear that condemns the woman to a cycle of violence.

CHAPTER 8

The Pimp:
Analytical Examination

Illusion of Protection

A critical analysis of the role of pimps is required to fully understand the characteristics of the pimp-prostitute relationship. This chapter explores the role and function of pimps to reveal how pimps generate employment strategies by monopolizing on violence. The imagery and hierarchial structures of pimps are examined. This chapter concludes by offering a subcultural social typology of pimps to expose some common qualities, similarities and disparities.

Pimps advise prostitutes that they need protection on the street. Pimps advocate that they will protect them from all the evils of the street. Analysis of this claim of protection allows one to recognize that pimps have set up an enterprise in which they have created a demand for their own services. When prostitutes are being beaten by a bad date, pimps are usually not physically present to protect them. When they are being arrested by the police, pimps are usually the first people scrambling to leave the scene. One must ask, then, just who or what do pimps protect prostitutes from? The only protection that pimps can provide is protection from other pimps or people acting under their direction. Pimps use acts of threats, assaults and other methods of persuasion to obligate prostitutes to acquire and to need the services of pimps. Karen and Carol respectively report their experiences in attempting to work as prostitutes without the attachment to a pimp:

> When I left Martin [pimp], I tried to work on my own. Pimps kept walking and driving by and kept asking, "Who's your man?" Many of the other girls kept asking also.... Usually

within two days, I would get jacked up by some pimp or by one of the other girls.

Interview: Sixteen-year-old: April 17, 1990

You couldn't work on the stroll without a man. Everyone would ask you, I mean it's impossible to be on the stroll without a man. Even if you said that so and so was your man, the pimps would take your money and say, "Tell so and so to come and see me to get his money." Of course since you didn't have some one, the pimp would know you didn't have a man and would be back within a couple of days to make you work for him.

Interview: Seventeen-year-old: April 17, 1990

If a prostitute does not acquire a pimp's service, she risks an increased chance of being "jacked up" (robbed) by pimps or by other working girls who are directed by their own pimps to rob the girls who do not have a "man." Pimps protect women from other pimps just like themselves and the exploitive process continues.

Illusion of Soliciting Clients

Most dictionaries define a pimp as "a man who solicits clients for a prostitute." This assertion is never realized in the self-reports or in the observational reports. It appears that pimps do not participate in the soliciting role, as this is clearly within the prostitute's job description. P.J., a convicted pimp, discloses:

Pimps don't get no customers for the girls, what guy in his right mind is going to go with a pimp to get a prostitute.... A customer won't stop his car even if he sees ten or twenty prostitutes standing around when a pimp is there.

Interview: Twenty-four-year-old: July 2, 1987

D.C., another pimp, reports:

No pimps don't get Johns, they can't get Johns, I mean how is he going to get Johns.... The Johns want to see the

merchandise, right. Buyer beware and smart shopping and all
that stuff, right. It just doesn't happen that way, I mean that's
the Hoe's job, not mine.

Interview: Eighteen-year-old: December 6,1988

Most clients of prostitutes do not risk their own safety by becoming so engulfed
or close to the street subculture that they themselves could become victim to a
pimp's violence. All evidence clearly suggests that a pimp does not engage in
the endeavour of soliciting clients for prostitutes. This misrepresented role of
the pimp only further fosters an increased level of illusionary perception
regarding the strategies of pimps.

Imagery and Hierarchy: To Be a "Mack"

Pimps are assisted in their game within the pimp-prostitute subculture by
an image and a network consisting of a pimp hierarchy that enables them to
continue their manipulation and exploitation of women. Pimps are assisted in
these endeavours by "players" who, according to Kenny, are "apprentice pimps"
or "pimps in training." Mitchell (1984:109) in her study, cites that "pimps learn
to be successful through other pimps." Ace reports:

When I started out, I worked for Johnny for almost a year,
like I did a lot of his dirty work, like discipline, collecting and
things. He taught me the game. He showed the ins and outs,
so to speak, I learned fast. Johnny started giving me more
responsibility and eventually he gave me a Hoe that was
trying to chump him off. I started working her and eventually
I went out on my own.

Interview: Seventeen-year-old: June 6, 1986

William disclosed that:

Yea, I had three players working for me at one time. They
helped me out a lot with the things you got to do. I've had
some good ones. Usually they are good, I mean you hand
pick them, they got to see things your way. They are working
up to getting their own business so they have to learn, like

an apprentice or something. Sometimes you have to pull them in because they get too ambitious, but they can take a lot of heat off you.

Interview: Twenty-eight-year-old: March 10, 1987

Players are responsible for assisting pimps in procuring and exercising control of prostitutes. Players cannot become pimps until they have worked as a player for a period of time and have received the pimp's trust and respect. Players are given some monetary payment from pimps and are eventually given a prostitute to "turn-out" and thus acquire the position of pimp.

Often it is the players who are detailed to watch the prostitutes on the "stroll," collect the money, administer the discipline and provide support for pimps when in conflict with other pimps. It is interesting that there are very few reports of pimps who actually engage in physical confrontations with each other; however, it is obvious how pimps indirectly batter each other. Pimps settle disputes with each other by inflicting violence on and robbing each other's prostitutes. Johnny explains:

Yea, man, you got to be careful, I mean you can't go around beating each other up. You got to go were its going to hurt the most. I mean this game is about making coin, and if you want to hurt a guy, take out his coin generating device.

Interview: Twenty-year-old: June 18, 1986

A pimp who is having difficulties with another pimp physically beats the other pimp's prostitutes. The prostitute is often unable to work as her face may be extremely bruised or she is severely injured. This action only reconfirms the pimp's position of being required to provide the prostitute with protection on the street.

The factors that determine where pimps would be positioned within the hierarchy are such issues as the number of prostitutes that a pimp controls, the number of players employed, the possession of material items and the ability to command and receive respect on the street. Simone reports:

It's all part of the game. You've got to look and feel the part, the image. You've got to command respect on the street and if it looks like you are making it, you get respect big time. If you look like you are losing, they will treat you like a loser. You've got to flash the cash and let people see the things you have to let them think that you've got everything and not a worry in the world.

Interview: Twenty-two-year-old male: April 15, 1987

Judy, a former wife-in-law, explains this posturing within the hierarchy:

Ah yea man, they'd be strolling for you.... Showing you their goods and acting important and all. I mean, it's part of the role. You got to look and act successful. If people think you are successful they treat you good. You've got to keep up the image. It's so important.

Interview: Twenty-one-year-old: August 2, 1988

These factors allow pimps to reinforce the imagery that is portrayed by the media and other sources and they grant pimps the liberty to continue with their pursuit to climb the hierarchical ladder to acquire the status of the "mack" (top pimp). If pimps are to reach this plateau, they must be committed to "play the game" with vigour and tyranny.

Cultural Implications: Generating a Social Typology

A subcultural social typology of pimps is further offered in an attempt to identify common qualities, similarities and disparities of the individuals who become involved in pimping. The data to be administered within this context are obtained from observations in the field and police records of arrests.

The imagery that this pimp subculture elicits has severe cultural implications in portraying race and gender as a factor. The street subculture appears to highlight distinctions of success, or perceived success, based along racial and gender lines. Apparent societal, racial and gender expectations and the street subcultural depiction certainly suggest that skin colour and gender may be exercised as a factor. This street subcultural depiction appears to suggest that "black males" may more readily fit societal expectations of what a pimp looks like and subsequently what the street subculture expects and demands. The societal and street imagery appear to display a romanticized concept of young black males with extraordinary capabilities of operationalizing "the game" and subsequently obtaining material items, an enhanced street status, the freedom of being your own boss and, specifically, not working for white employers.

The implications of this imagery are such that some young black males may view this pimp subculture as a most acceptable and intriguing lifestyle. It certainly provides for a method in which to realize societal cultural goals, monetary gain and status enhancement. Moreover, it provides institutional means to realize societal cultural goals outside of the mundane and often subservient existence of being employed by institutions that pay minimum wages and generate minimum social status. Eddy and Doug highlight the cultural emphases within the pimping subculture:

> This is it. What else can a guy do? What else would you want to do? Bros like me don't get no job anywhere else. I mean, I'd be just a bum boy, getting this and that. I'd just be a regular poor nigger. But this way I demand and get respect. I got the white bitches working for me and I get the money from the white johns. Now ain't that justice.... I mean look at the things I got. My clothes, my car. Shit man, I got more things then half the people in my hood.
>
> *Interview: Twenty-eight-year-old: June 10, 1987*

> You ain't going to get anywhere being a black man unless you play the game. I mean what am I going to do, work at McDonalds? Come on... I mean for the most part people assume you're playing the game as soon as you arrive on the street. People think that because you are black that you are either a pimp or a drug dealer, or both. The girls expect you to be black. I mean there are some white guys around trying to play the game but skin colour becomes an issue. The white guys can't be taken seriously. Most of the white guys are working the hoes through escorts or strip clubs... I guess they can't handle the heat of the street.
>
> *Interview: Twenty-year-old: September 28, 1988*

Karen, a wife-in-law, also highlights the cultural emphasis of the street:

> Most of the movers and shakers are the bros. They are good at the business.... There are some white guys trying to push the girls, but for the most part they are not taken seriously.

They just don't fit in or get the respect. Most of them are afraid of the bros.

Interview: Twenty-three-year-old: July 10, 1990

Heather, who worked as a prostitute, reported similar experiences:

I always worked for the black guys. They were the ones taking the game seriously. I mean, they played the part, lived the part, breathed the part. They usually walked the talk. There were some white guys involved but for the most part they were full of shit. No one took them seriously. They were usually afraid of the black pimps.

Interview: Seventeen-year-old: June 28, 1988

The young black males, with few social options available to them, are most likely to find this romanticized pimping subculture very appealing.

The possible impact and inducing aspects of this subculture on young black males is illustrated in a letter, which a pimp who had been convicted of pimping activities and subsequently sentenced to several years in prison wrote. This letter was introduced as evidence at a court of appeal in which the pimp describes the possible reasons for his involvement in pimping. The letter reads:

...I now intend to give you reasons why I began to pimp, although I have not come to a full understanding as to the reasons. I suspect that the main reason is ignorance. That is, on the surface I eulogized pimping. It was especially popular among blacks. At the time when I got involved in pimping I had just gone through a stage of my youth called "the fly guy era." This stage can be considered similar to the "punk rock era," based on fanaticism, though a great number of the customs differ. Specifically, fly guys listen to rap music, break dance and party all and every weekend. The fly guys performance of these activities are, in part, judged by the number of girls he picks up. Since the fly guy comes from a poor to middle-class family, his parents can hardly afford to support his often extravagant lifestyle. But that's alright, because the fly guy's ability to shoplift and have a finesse at petty crimes is another characteristic. It is these activities that led me downtown, the main gathering place of the fly guys.

Here, much of our time is spent picking up girls and shoplifting. It is also where the fly guys see the easy lifestyle of the pimp. He doesn't have to worry about getting arrested for shoplifting and serving time. Pimping to some extent is a direct complement of the lifestyle of the fly guy. This, and the fact that the fly guys look up to the pimp, makes the pull towards pimping that much stronger.

When I made that ill-fated mistake and graduated to pimping, my only intent was to get money needed to party, attend clubs, buy expensive clothing and jewellery. I had no intentions on hurting anyone, and certainly never gave a great deal of consideration to the consequences and effects of my actions. In terms of morals and basic values, my view at the time was, "If the girl wanted to work, what was the big deal. She would only end up working for someone else anyways. Why not me?" Essentially, it was this ignorance on my part that led to my ill-fated decision to become a pimp.

Once I made this critical mistake and got involved in pimping, my personality changed dramatically. I found myself caught up in the prostitution game. All my acquaintances were pimps and prostitutes. In a way, I became brainwashed by the older pimps, listening to their stories about the best methods to "exercise their game." Under these conditions it became very easy for me to do things I wouldn't ordinarily have done. I became so caught up in this "game" that it was not until I was arrested that I fully realized and began to understand what I was doing or more appropriately what I had done.

It is clear within the context of this letter that the individual entered the pimping subculture after being influenced by the imagery that the subculture displayed. This appeal would most likely have a tremendous impact on young men who are marginalized in society.

The imagery enhancing cultural implications is also represented in some of the "rap music" that some young pimps set forth. The following lyrics were written by two young pimps. The lyrics were used as evidence in court to display several images that are presented with reference to cultural emphasis. The lyrics are to be expressed in the rap fashion and are as follows:

FOXY

My name is foxy, and I like to rock
All white bitches want to suck my cock
I am tall, and I'm lean
To those bitches I am so mean
Remember back in history
White people had nigers in slavery
Now this is the 1980s
I was born to pimp white ladies
I have a voice that is so sweet
When I sing all the ladies weep
I use that for my control
To put those honkies on the stroll
They have to give me lots of money
Just for a taste of my buddy
I have no feelings for those bitches
If it were my way they'd be digging ditches
Workin all hours with no pay
That's how I think, I feel no way.

SPARKY

My name is Sparky, or don't you know
I don't have a girl, I have a hoe
All women want to be with me
Cause I'm a nigger with versatility
I'm short, I'm sweet, I'm one of a kind
I'm so bad I'll blow your mind
I've got class and I've got style
I'll rock you women for awhile
To you over there, you might be cute
dressed up in a bright pink suit
With curly hair and bright blue eyes
You could never please this guy
You walk around like you are high class
Do that near me and I'll kick your ass
Just because you cute, don't be bold
Cause I'm one nigger who'll knock you cold.

There are indeed clear references within these lyrics to cultural standing, which are used to present the image of black people exercising power and control over white people. Jennifer and Kathy reported the continuous racial references that are exercised within this subculture:

> Johnny would always call us his white bitches. He used to always call us his sex slaves and say that things have changed so much for black people. All the pimps would say things about white hoes working for the black man or that the black man is king and stuff like that.
>
> *Interview: Seventeen-year-old: May 19, 1989*

> We were just white trash to them [the pimps]. They would always tell you that and say you are working for the black man now so you have to show respect. They always said black was better and black was beautiful. Adrian would always say "once you had black there ain't no going back".... They were always putting you down and telling you ain't shit because you are white.
>
> *Interview: Eighteen-year-old: January 10, 1990*

Again, these extremely powerful images and attitudes may result in black males viewing the pimping subculture as an alternative to being subservient to white people.

The romanticized display of this world of pimping in terms of the achievement of material items, the opportunity to be eulogized, social status within the culture, power over people, power over white people and, more specifically, power over white females may be extremely enticing. The images of pimping clearly portray many black men who are perceived to be extremely powerful and respected on the street and do not have to answer to the white man. The pimping subculture's ability to display this imagery fosters involvement of many individuals who have very few social opportunities or conditions available to them. The cultural implications on a class of people in North American society who are often without social opportunities are that they will likely choose to become involved in the pimping subculture, which appears to afford an opportunity for advancement in society.

Observations made in the field corroborate the self-reports in suggesting that black "street" pimps are by far more prevalent in proportion to the number of white street pimps. This unequal racial distribution may be due to the impact that the pimp imagery has within black youth cultures, but there may be other reasons for this apparent disproportionate distribution. This study does not purport that all pimps are black, but it strongly suggests that the majority of pimps involved in the street sex trade are black. These findings can be explained by conducting an analysis of the sex trade hierarchical ladder. The upper end of this ladder supports the escort services and the bottom end sustains the street sex trade. The escort services are usually a more profitable, cleaner, less visible, "behind closed doors" prostitution system and are usually administered by white males. The white males' enhanced position within the sex trade hierarchy enables them to perform their functions behind closed doors and out of the sight of the police and public. In contrast, the street sex trade appears to be managed predominately by black males. The black males have to conduct their business on the street, which makes them extremely visible to the police and the public. The high visibility of black males operating as pimps on the street portrays an image that only black males are involved in pimping. In reality, white males are pimps, but they are not as visible to the police and public.

Several strong correlations could be made within conventional society as to who holds the jobs. This analysis is offered in an attempt to distinguish why there may be an over abundance of black males working as street pimps. Within the street pimp subculture, many black males are overrepresented. In North American society, there are many examples within the conventional work force of black men traditionally performing the jobs that are on the bottom of the employment hierarchial ladder. The males performing as sex trade managers in the escort system can be correlated to the conventional workforce to distinguish who holds the jobs that are at the top. Generally speaking most of the workers at the top are white men and there are very few black males in these more favourable employment positions. Unequal educational and occupational opportunities or conditions within North American society, combined with the street pimp imagery, are seen here as contributing factors that may direct young black males to become involved in pimping. Young black males may be forced to adapt to this environment of inequality of condition and opportunity by employing street survival methods. These street survival methods may include such activities as theft, drug dealing, break and enter, robbing, pimping and other criminal offences. For some young black males who are close to or aware of this street subculture, the notion of becoming a street pimp may be the only perceived option that their environment affords.

Social-Economic Status

Many of these pimps are coming from within lower socioeconomic class structures. Both the black and white street pimps seemed to be from a lower socioeconomic class. If the man is not from a family of lower socioeconomic class position, then he quickly engenders this status when he tries to live on his own and compete for employment in urban centres. The abandonment of a familiar setting usually results in the abandonment of any academic aspirations. The average highest level of education achieved by the pimps assessed within this study is Grade Ten. This failure to complete formal schooling adds to the plight of these men in their attempts to obtain gainful employment in the conventional workforce. Many of them are unemployed, unskilled and virtually unemployable. They quickly invoke street survival methods and attempt to maintain an existence by whatever means are available and necessary.

Age

The ages of the pimps under study vary; with the youngest fifteen years of age and the oldest forty-five years of age. The overall average age of the street pimps is the early twenties. There appears to be strong correlations between the age of pimps and the age of the prostitutes that pimps have working for them. The younger pimps have younger prostitutes working for them and older pimps have older prostitutes. This correlation may be attributed to the seduction method of procurement in which the young pimp's original success may be dependent on the young woman's physical attraction to the young pimp. The instances of a young woman being physically attracted to an older pimp are rare.

Street Status

The age of pimps also correlates with their status within the pimping subculture. Younger pimps are often referred to as "popcorn pimps." These popcorn pimps are viewed as individuals who do not yet understand the pimp game. Pimps who reach the "Mack" status are older and have been playing the game for many years. There are obvious advantages to surviving the rigours of several years of pimping. The pimps' age and experience assist them to achieve elevated status within the subculture.

The popcorn pimps are at the bottom of the hierarchial ladder and the Mack pimps are at the top. In between these two extremes are pimps attempting to maintain an existence. The popcorn pimps are new to the prostitution game but are striving to upgrade their status. The other pimps are also attempting to enhance their status which is determined by the number of prostitutes they have working for them, the acquisition of material items and the ability to command respect on the street.

Gender

The dominance of the male gender within the subculture is extremely evident. This unequal distribution may be the characteristic of the blatant form of dominant sexist ideologies that this subculture endorses and demands. It feeds on the ability of men to physically and psychologically coerce women. There are a few examples in which women are seen to be performing the role of the pimps on the street; however, closer examination usually reveals that they have the benefit of utilizing men to assist them with the prostitution game. The female pimp can call upon these men to incorporate physical punishment or threaten bothersome rivals. The dominance of men and the subservience of women are the basis in which this subculture exists and flourishes.

Conclusion

A critical analysis of the role of pimps reveals many characteristics of the pimp-prostitute relationship and provides a subcultural social typology of pimps and their relations with prostitutes, other pimps and players. This examination reveals that pimps do indeed provide protection for street prostitutes, but the protection is established to guard against other pimps who are diligently attempting to acquire the prostitute's money and employment opportunities. Therefore, pimps have set up an enterprise in which they have created a demand for their own services. The data clearly highlight that pimps do not participate in soliciting potential clients but spend much of their time generating fear and establishing creditability on the street.

Pimps employ a hierarchy on the street to determine and enhance their image as keen, prudent, tough and shrewd entrepreneurs. Pimps utilize apprentice pimps, often called players, and wives-in-law to assist with the day-to-day management of the street sex trade. This division of labour allows pimps to operate with greater certainty and creditability. The many factors that ascertain where a pimp is positioned within the hierarchy include the number of prostitutes working for him, the number of players involved, possession of material items and the aptitude to secure respect on the street.

The imagery that this subculture portrays has tempestuous implications for cultural and racial expressions. Young men who find themselves in positions with few social or economic opportunities will most likely find this subculture exceedingly intriguing and accessible. Specifically, social and subcultural images and expectations detail stereotypical expressions for young black men who may find themselves marginalized. This results in an overrepresentation of black males operating as street sex trade managers. The data suggest that whites may be overrepresented as sex trade managers within escort agencies and other less visible methods of operationalizing sex for money services.

The data demonstrate that street pimps often come from lower socioeconomic class circumstances and, on average, accomplish a Grade Ten education level, and may be considered as unemployable within the conventional workplace. The age of the pimps varies, however strong correlations are reported between the age of the pimp and the age of the prostitute under his command. The pimps who were older and more firmly established on the street receive considerable respect and status. The data also exhibit that the male gender certainly dominates the pimping role and extreme measures of masculinity are often expressed in the form of demanding that women play subservient roles. This analytical examination of the role of pimps allows for an enhanced understanding of the complexities of the roles that pimps play within this subculture. Pimps have set up a system to produce and reproduce prostitution ideology and practices within this street subculture.

CHAPTER 9

Policing the Game:
Social Service/Law Enforcement
and the Street Sex Trade

The street sex trade and its complexities generate many problematic considerations for social services and law enforcement officials. The institutional responses vary with many programs designed and developed to address issues relating to the street sex trade. This chapter highlights the characteristics of programs that respond to the needs of the adolescents involved in street prostitution. Specifically this chapter utilizes a case study approach to illustrate programs within the social service and law enforcement mandates.

Social Service Response:
Mandated Teen Services

Many of the social services program changes began in 1984 and 1985 in a response to the increasing quantity of young prostitutes in many urban centres, as well as the visibly greater number of teens under sixteen years of age working as prostitutes. It was clear, at the time, that conventional interventions used by social service agencies and police departments were not substantially impacting on this age group. Subsequently, these teens were becoming entrenched in a lifestyle cycle characterized by chronic running away from home, prostitution and the associated dangers of physical and mental health issues. The social services programs under study for this effort highlight a change in philosophy of care and an emphasis on a continuous holistic inclusive approach to address the needs of "kids in crisis."

A greater emphasis on "mandated services" for teen prostitutes was one of the factors that departed from existing programs in the 1980s. Prevailing child care philosophy of the time felt that, in order to have a positive impact on teen prostitution, intervention must be of a "voluntary nature." It was advocated that the child must be motivated to make voluntary choices to seek intervention. There is little doubt that the "voluntary nature" emphasis would certainly enhance any intervention model; however, it is often a characteristic denied those working with troubled children and adolescents in crisis.

As indicated earlier, the motivation to leave the prostitution environment is often generated by such factors as fear, exhaustion and feelings of betrayal, loneliness and being used. Traumatic incidents such as being seriously assaulted can also motivate a voluntary retreat from the street. Although a significant number of women leave the streets because of these factors, many others do not. The problem, as the new mandated services articulate, is dealing with a clientele who are first adolescent; second, often very emotionally disturbed; and third, and maybe most important, socially isolated and largely alienated from social norms and values. The young person's immersion into prostitution creates and establishes new norms, values and beliefs, which the child has internalized. It can be argued that most adolescents feel immortal and invincible and, in that respect, adolescent prostitutes are no different. The significant difference is in the atmosphere and manner in which teen prostitutes lead their lives. As indicated earlier, "life on the track" involves high risk behaviour and factors that most certainly can lead to early mortality; however, very few of the adolescent prostitutes perceive or acknowledge the risks generated by street life.

The emphasis on "mandated services" is grounded in the principle that children are involved in extremely risky, destructive and degrading behaviour. Therefore, it is argued that intervention programs must be intrusive to remove the child at the earliest point and impede them from their risky and destructive lifestyle. Yaworski (1986:5) acknowledges this necessity to focus on mandated intervention:

> These kids are involved in an extremely dangerous lifestyle, and playing the games by the rules is a survival tactic and seeking a way off the street is not playing by the rules.... Little in this scenario [prostitution] contributes to motivating kids to leave the street on their own. Although all likely consider escaping for brief moments, it seems impossible and their lives

off the streets offer too many uncertainties. Returning to a life of physical or sexual abuse, school problems, or parental neglect are not viable alternatives and until recently authorities failed to take a long, hard look at the lives these kids chose first to escape.... So when these resistant, angry, scared, and often out-of-control kids arrive at [phase one— mandated services centre], their willingness and co-operation are secondary issues. As child welfare authorities, our primary consideration is their safety and physical and emotional well-being.

Within the mandated services model, the intake regimen is purposely intrusive and socially necessary to stabilize out-of-control kids. This level of intrusion is certainly well grounded in most juvenile courts and is based on the legal concept of *"parens patriae." Parens patriae* is an old English doctrine that sanctioned the right of the state to intervene into natural family relations whenever a child's welfare was threatened.

The Rights of Children

The greater emphasis on apprehending children involved in risky behaviour was seen by some child-care professionals, in the early 1980s, as too great of an encroachment on the rights of the child. This apparent infringement on "individual sovereignty" of children was, of course, weighed against the concept of the "public or societal good." The question being debated at the time was whether or not the public good was so threatened that the individual rights of children had to be abrogated or eroded. As more information became available as to the destructive and dangerous environments in which children were living while involved in prostitution, many child-care advocates agreed that greater emphasis must be weighted towards the protection of society and thus the protection of children. There was an enhanced understanding of the circumstances that motivate children into this lifestyle, but also the problematic features of trying to get kids out became much more obvious. Moreover, the change in focus to view the "child as victim" provided a catapult for arguing for substantial interventive powers. The "child as victim" philosophy depicted these adolescents as victims of dysfunctional home environments and, subsequently, interactions with school, peers and state authorities were marginalized. These children were emotionally and physically in acute danger and were seen as "children at risk" to themselves and to society and, therefore, were children in need of protection. Obviously, the child's home environment was unable to provide the stability or protection necessary; therefore, it is incumbent on the state to provide the protection needed to ensure safety for this vulnerable group.

There is little doubt that voluntary intervention has extreme merit in establishing effective programs to meet the needs of clients. However, it is argued here that the prostitute client base has extremely compound factors that, for the most part, limit the effectiveness of voluntary intervention. Due to the prostitute's deep level of immersion into this subculture and her subsequent attachment and reliance on her pimp, these clients are extremely difficult to motivate utilizing a voluntary context. Specifically, intervention programs can not and will not work if there is no access to clients. The prostitution environment demands subcultural control and isolation and rebuffs any "outside" voluntary intrusion or intervention. It is argued, therefore, that in order to get access to this endangered marginalized client base extreme levels of intrusion must be mandated to intercept, assess, stabilize and provide treatment for these victims.

Toronto Street Youth Project

The "mandated services to teen prostitutes" model to be highlighted here is one operationalized in Toronto, Ontario, Canada. This program works under the title of the Toronto Street Youth Project. The project maintains a focus on the principle of preserving the status of "victim" for child prostitutes and focuses on intervention, apprehension, identification, assessment, medical care and emotional and physical stabilization.

Phase one of the Toronto Street Youth Project is the reception centre to which these at-risk kids are admitted. Again, these kids have to be apprehended by police or other child welfare workers and brought to the centre for admission. Intake forms are filled out, documenting relevant information about families, recent activities, physical health and emotional condition at time of admission. The teens are photographed and then required to shower using disinfectant shampoo. Their personal possessions are recorded and stored until their discharge. They are given pyjamas to wear and fed if they are hungry. The facility is locked from the outside to prevent entry of the unwanted public, but more importantly, the staff prevent the teens from leaving since the young people are seen as at risk and their unscheduled departure will put them at greater risk. Yaworski (1986:5) reports on the success of phase one:

> The success, however, comes from the nurturing, care, and acceptance that follow. Such basics as being properly fed, wearing clean clothes, and sleeping alone in a clean, warm bed have tremendous impact. Even more powerful is being in an atmosphere which is relatively non-judgemental and which encourages kids to talk about life on the streets. Very few hookers or hustlers are not embarrassed about their involvement in prostitution. Clad in luminous spandex, many still deny being a hooker, but abandon their denial when they realize that all other residents are hookers. Staff are accepting, affectionate, and firm with residents and the result is usually a sense of relief and safety brought about by being off the tightrope for the first time in perhaps months. That is not to say that given the opportunity many would not run.... The surprise, however, is the increasing number of teens admitted involuntarily, who return later as self-referrals. As well, many who are returned by police are much more positive the second time around (or third, or fourth...). The conclusion drawn from this is that the program which initially only seems restrictive and punitive, comes to be seen as a place that is safe and welcoming. For some it's a place to escape, for others a place to rest. One of the principles of child care is that children and adolescents whose lives lack structure and control require limits and consistency from responsible, accountable adults. The result is usually a feeling of safety and the creation of a climate in which they can talk about the events in their past which have contributed to the chaotic lives they now lead. The approach I've described is basically good parenting. Making major choices like deciding to leave the street requires maturity and a degree of objectivity. A fifteen-year-old runaway with an unhappy background, performing oral sex on strangers, for money, six times a day, is in no position to

make such a choice. There is another urgent factor in working with teen hookers that makes a quick response vital. Ill health, manifested by malnutrition and venereal disease, is rampant among this group of kids. Their systems are generally run-down by the lack of regular sleep or a balanced diet, making them more susceptible to colds, flu, and infection.

The young people are moved to phase two within two days, where they are assessed for a thirty- to ninety-day period. Phase two of the program emphasizes respect for the young person, caring, nurturing and openness along with clear expectations. Kochendorfer (1986:1) reports:

> The purpose of the program [phase two] is to provide a short-term stabilization and assessment period for children living on the "streets" generally involved in prostitution. The expected length of stay is up to eight weeks. During that time the young person's physical, emotional, educational, and medical needs are attended.

Kochendorfer (1986:1) further highlights the programming details:

> The program is highly structured with a high ratio of staff to residents. The core structure comes from a behaviourial management program that incorporates points and levels. This program allows the young person to quickly incorporate into the program by clearly understanding behaviourial expectations. It helps create a setting in which individual goals can be pursued. The individual goals and techniques for handling each youth's behaviour are set in conjunction with the youth's social workers from other agencies.... Group discussions around house issues and planning, problems common to the youth, and various living skills and current issues are an integral part of the program. The youths attend a school on site. They are provided ongoing medical attention by our house doctor and nurse. The youths remain involved with the community through recreational activities, i.e., library excursions, fruit picking, swimming and volunteer outings to movies and bowling.

The issue of prostitution is dealt with openly yet with a consciousness of confidentiality. Through group discussion and one-on-one conversations with staff, the youths are able to discuss the pros and cons of street life without fear of rejection or embarrassment. This allows the youths to support one another in their attempts to exit the streets. This also generates an atmosphere of working towards common goals and the ability to confront those who would otherwise brag or be misleading about the streets.

Based on the belief that the youths first have to deal with their identification as a "hooker," then their own individual problem areas, these issues are immediately confronted. We have found that by dealing openly with their hooking we can then get the youths to be more global in identifying their problem areas. Once this is accomplished, problem solving around each problem area can occur. We feel this approach accounts for the success in youths remaining in the program and stabilizing. Many of the youths are then ready to share their concerns with others. One positive result from this project is the sharing of information by youths with the police. The police handle these issues very sensitively and have found the information valuable in laying charges against the pimps. This action reflects the sense of safety the young person feels and a desire to exit prostitution.

The basic philosophy and specific goals of the program are that the children must be respected and accepted as individuals with positive assets and potential. The philosophy embraces a notion that when the young people rid themselves of the barriers erected by their milieu, they have an inner striving towards growth and actualization. When these barriers are dismantled and problem-solving skills put into place, the youth can make meaningful steps forward in life. The program recognizes that it is impractical to think great strides can be made in this direction during a short-term stay; however, this philosophy arises in the attitude of the workers to the youth and the direction taken with problem-solving and goal attainment. The specific goals of the program are outlined in Kochendorfer in noting:

1) To receive children in need of care and assessment and children on probation with an order to reside.

2) To detain these children when applicable.
3) To provide interim daily care and nurturance.
4) To support the young person in a crisis period.
5) To assist the youth in developing problem-solving skills.
6) To allow the youths time and assistance in reflecting on their immediate situation and in planning long-term goals.
7) To work towards goals as set out in the centre's plan of care.
8) To instill a respect for one's own personal and legal rights and respect for the rights of others.
9) To offer an experience in the give and take of group interaction.
10) To maintain, as much as is practical, the individual's relatedness to his or her community including the encouragement of family contacts where feasible.
11) To assess the behaviour of the resident while at the centre and contribute to the overall assessment needs of the child.
12) To provide input into case conferences.
13) Where applicable, to share knowledge and insight gained about the child with his or her next placement.
14) To be an advocate for the child so that his or her rights are protected, his or her voice is heard, and his or her best interests are pursued. (Kochendorfer 1986:1)

The phase two level of programming empowers the children to take control of their lives and begin their journey of making healthy life choices. Phase three includes the child being placed in an appropriate treatment facility, group home, foster home or, in some cases, returned home.

Law Enforcement Response: Juvenile Task Force

As disclosed, many social service agencies had to rethink and redevelop programs that addressed the distinct needs of young people involved in prostitution. A number of law enforcement institutions were struggling with similar issues in regards to how to effectively respond to this group of out-of-control kids that appeared to be arriving on the street in unprecedented numbers. Police departments in Canada and the United States established juvenile speciality units to assess and develop policies that would provide an adequate police response to this emerging crisis in urban centres.

The law enforcement model to be examined here is the establishment and development of a unit by the Metropolitan Toronto Police Department called the Juvenile Task Force. The Juvenile Task Force was comprised of six plain-clothes police officers under the supervision of a criminal investigative bureau sergeant. It was developed in the early 1980s after members of the community, public officials, social service agencies and police administrators became increasingly aware of and concerned about the magnitude of adolescents from Metropolitan Toronto, as well as those from other areas of Canada and the United States, who were continuously attracted to the downtown core of the city of Toronto. Specifically, political and social pressure was calling for increased police response to child welfare developments that were emerging in many social services agencies. The Juvenile Task Force was formed because of these concerns.

The primary purpose of the unit was the identification, investigation, apprehension and prosecution of youthful offenders and adult organizers. The secondary function was the dissemination and distribution of information to specialized units within the community, the police force and other law enforcement agencies in Canada and the United States. The distribution of information to child welfare agencies detailed strong and close working arrangements between this police unit and the many social services departments in the area. These close ties mandated that this police unit had to adopt and adapt untraditional approaches to providing police services.

The juvenile task force began receiving many complaints from women who reported that they had been approached by men and asked to work as prostitutes. It also discovered that an increasing amount of runaway juveniles were becoming involved in prostitution. This awareness resulted in the force conducting surveillance and investigations into the prostitute and pimp relationships in Canada and parts of the United States—at the street level. This type of investigation has allowed the force to specialize in adolescent prostitution.

This specialization resulted in research that quickly illustrated that most adolescents were not running away from their residences or other places of abode with the intention of becoming involved in prostitution. When these young women arrived in many urban centres across North America, they were being procured into prostitution by adult organizers, namely pimps, who were active throughout urban centres. The force also observed an unprecedented influx of pimps operating on the streets of downtown Toronto and other large cities. It related that this increased presence of pimps was directly responsible for the growing incidence of adolescent prostitution.

Members of the force assessed the relationship between pimps and young prostitutes as an intolerable form of child abuse and sexual exploitation. These pimps cultivate and exploit the young runaway's vulnerabilities, her low self-esteem, her loneliness on the street and her need for love and protection. These pimps are actively oppressing the environment in which these young runaways are compelled to work and robbing these young women of their human dignity and of opportunities for pursuing a more healthful and constructive way of life. These pimps view runaway children as economic assets. The younger children are more desirable to pimps for several reasons: runaways are not in control of their lives (i.e., problems at home); they have no means of support; they are in unfamiliar environments (no accommodation); they have no agency to turn to for support, (i.e., on the run and under sixteen); and they are easier to exercise control over and influence. These pimps seek out the weak and vulnerable, which are, all to often, the runaway juveniles.

The task force has become very involved in the investigation of these pimps, which has resulted in several serious criminal charges being laid. Young runaways are being located due to the investigation and surveillance of these pimps. The task force members believe that investigating and removing pimps from the streets has had, and will continue to have, an immeasurable effect on the crime picture in urban centres. However, members of this unit began to recognize that the reliance on criminal charges to regulate the actions of runaways was failing miserably.

The Juvenile Task Force began to reconsider it's approach to utilizing criminal legislation to control young people who were experiencing personal crisis. It was most apparent that these children were leaving their places of abode because of a dysfunctional home environment, only to arrive on the street to be seduced or coerced into prostitution. Often when the young person was charged with criminal offences, such as prostitution-related offences, the young person began to accumulate other offences such as failing to comply with probation order, failing to appear in court, obstructing justice and obstructing the police. The utilization of criminal charges began to be seen as not only ineffective in curtailing the activities of this distinct group of young people, but often serving to further compound and bond these young people to greater reliance on the street subculture.

Relying fully on criminal sanctions to change behaviour became more and more problematic as it appeared to have a limited effect and seemed to further destabilize young people. The unit's close ties with the social service agencies and its specialization into this social site allowed it to maintain that the child prostitute should be seen as the victim of home and street circumstances and was only further victimized by criminal charges and official labelling of criminality. This recognition detailed that it was necessary for the task force to develop untraditional approaches to address the needs of this vulnerable group of young people. This untraditional approach maintained the utilization of child welfare legislation to empower the police to apprehend children in need of protection and take them to a place of safety.

The abandonment of a criminal focus as a method of operationalizing and visualizing police services was not an easy attainment. Members of this unit had to embrace and combine principles of law enforcement, the social sciences and social service philosophies to meet the needs of this street community. For many members of the force, this transition was most difficult and required much work to challenge their "favourite ways of thinking and doing." The key to this transition was the ability of members to see these children as victims. This transitory process was difficult for most but was realized after utilizing social science models of providing a critical analysis of the children's social environment. The social science analysis enabled members to recognize that these young people did not just wake up one morning, decide to be hookers and go downtown to start turning tricks. This critical, in-depth analysis illuminated the social forces and circumstances that generated a complex projection of events that occurred or were occurring in the young person's life that pushed them to street prostitution. Juvenile Task Force members began to observe significant and immediate positive results by operationalizing a child welfare model of apprehending and protecting at-risk children.

The change in focus certainly established that the police and social services agencies were now operating with shared philosophies and strategies to meet the needs of these children. The development and movement from a criminal investigation role towards a social service focus allowed these police officers to further specialize in meeting the needs of the community. The criminal investigative role was obviously counterproductive when applied to the social site of juvenile prostitution. There are significant distinctions drawn between the traditional criminal investigative "authoritarian" role and the social service "humanitarian" role in policing. Schonborn (1976:29) suggests:

> Authoritarian officers are traditionalists believing in the efficiency of force [and criminal charges], they are quick to pass judgement and are often formal and inflexible during conflict interventions.

The provision of training and education for police officers that highlights the benefits of the social service aspects ensures that the police meet the needs of all members of the community. The police officers assigned to the Juvenile Task Force came to realize that utilizing the social service role allowed them to display a genuine interest in being helpful to young people in crisis and is perfectly consistent with effective police work. Schonborn (1976:35) identifies that humanitarian social service peace-keepers embrace an ideology:

> Words are generally more effective than physical force during conflict regulation, and come close to the conception of police as philosophers, guides, and friends.

Schonborn (1976:30) provides a summary of the ideological characteristics of the two peace-keeper types:

> Authoritarian peace-keepers are characterized by formality, rigidity, closedness, overreaction (violence proneness) and rely on coercion, weapons, physical power, sharp-shooter expertise, traditional procedures and role behaviour. In contrast, the humanitarian peace-keepers are characterized by informality, flexibility, openness, underreaction (non-violence proneness) and rely on persuasion, words, normative power, social service expertise, innovative procedures and non-role behaviour.

This humanitarian approach to peace-keeping espouses a social service conflict resolution focus that appears to be most advantageous to police organizations and officers who desire to meet and adapt to the needs of all members of their communities.

Pimp Legislation

Members of the Juvenile Task Force certainly observed some of the benefits of utilizing alternative measures in policing. However, members of the unit believed that utilizing criminal legislation was the most effective method in identifying and apprehending the adult organizers of juvenile prostitution. The enforcement of criminal legislation directed towards pimp activities provides many difficulties for law enforcement officials. The inherent complexities of much of the legislation, the prevailing social myths and the reliance on young witnesses make the realities of a successful conviction somewhat implausible. However, members of the task force have gained some success in the courts after informing the public and the courts as to the realities involved in the world of pimping. This educational endeavour resulted in a change of public attitude and awareness and, subsequently, the administering of significant jail sentences by judges in criminal courts. The harsh sentences handed down by the judges demonstrate the court's abhorrence of the pimps' repugnant activities.

Much of the criminal legislation operates under the concept that a person will register a complaint with the police of being procured and controlled by a pimp. As disclosed in the preceding chapters, many prostitutes are not willing to disclose their involvement with pimps until significant counselling is conducted. Although they may be motivated to disclose information about pimps, they can decide at any time to change their evidence or decide not to give any evidence at all. This sudden reluctance of witnesses to cooperate can seriously impair the chances of a successful prosecution. The games that pimps play with the lives of young prostitutes are not often conducive to generating willing witnesses to testify in court. Law enforcement officials have to work with social service officials to motivate some type of disclosure. This disclosure process can take several days or months to develop; therefore, it can prove to be an extremely expensive investigation that may end in an acquittal because of a reluctant witness.

In many jurisdictions, prior to 1988, legislation required that no one could be convicted of procuring or exercising control upon the evidence of only one witness unless the evidence of that witness is corroborated by evidence that implicates the accused. Corroboration is defined as other evidence that is independent of original evidence. This legislation outlined that the word of one prostitute was not sufficient to invoke these criminal sanctions. The clause clearly suggested that prostitutes could not be trusted to tell the truth. Other independent evidence was needed to verify their stories, although one crown attorney pointed out that "these prostitutes are not Pauline McGovern type witnesses but they are sincere and believable." Experience illustrates that when these women gave evidence in court, most judges and juries found that they presented their evidence in a factual, graphic, sincere and extremely creditable manner. They often gave better evidence than most police officers.

The requirements of this legislative corroboration further escalated the cost of investigating these offences. To collect the needed corroboration, law enforcement officials were required to resort to technical investigative procedures, including electronic surveillance and visual surveillance, to gather independent evidence. The cost of such technical investigations is extremely high and, at times, would result in some investigations being discontinued because of economic factors.

The education of the public and the courts regarding the plight of the women involved with pimps and the creditability of their evidence has generated legislative reform to alleviate the legislative need for corroboration. The legislative reform echoed the words of many advocates that these young women are not sluts or fallen women; they are our children and are credible people who have been victimized by society and pimps. The elimination of the corroboration requirement indicated that policy makers were now viewing the prostitutes as victims and that they also wanted to bring pimps into the courts faster and cheaper.

Sentencing: Expert Evidence

If the prosecution results in a conviction, educating the bench (judges) becomes extremely important in order to achieve an adequate sentence. This is the opportunity for law enforcement officials to illustrate to the bench the complexities of the pimp-prostitute relationship, the victimization of the prostitute and the resulting difficulties experienced by law enforcement officials in enforcing pimp legislation. Assistant crown attorney Stan Berger (1987:6) notes:

> It is extremely important for the Crown Attorney's office to present evidence at sentencing to demonstrate the nature of the business [of being a pimp], the relationship of the pimp to the prostitute, participants in the business, relationships of pimps to pimps, effect of the pimp business in the community and the problems for law enforcement authorities.

Berger suggests that this evidence is crucial in order to give the bench an accurate reflection of the world of a pimp. He (1987:6) notes that this evidence will emphasize the aggravating and mitigating factors in the case; he lists these aggravating and mitigating factors as:

> age and background of the pimp's target, coercion by force or threats, sophistication of the scheme, counselling the

prostitute to commit other offences, exposure to venereal disease or pregnancy, interfering with crown witnesses, criminal record, stealing personal property from the girls as a mode of control, taking the prostitutes out of familiar surroundings, age of the offender, the work history of the offender, attempts by the offender to rehabilitate himself.

Members of the task force became very much involved in educating the bench by getting themselves proclaimed as expert witnesses. The expert witness status allowed the officers to give opinion evidence during the sentencing of accused pimps in order to provide the courts with a clearer picture of the severity of the prostitution scene and the role of the accused in operating his mandate. Juvenile task force members were required to utilize the social sciences' empirical methodological principles of inquiry to make sense of the prostitution scene and present this information to the courts. This type of expert testimony offered judges an accurate depiction of the prostitution environment to highlight the exploitive, degrading and destructive nature of this activity. This disclosure allows judges to issue sentences that reflect social and individual concerns and costs in regards to pimps operating in our communities. Subsequently, judges could issue lengthy prison sentences to reflect the public abhorrence to such activities.

Conclusion

This chapter reveals that social service and law enforcement institutions have adapted and adopted programs and methods to police the street sex trade. Specifically, social service institutions moved to a mandated child welfare model that demanded that child-care officials apprehend children at risk and take them to a place of safety. This change in philosophy recognized the extreme conditions and circumstances in which young people were finding themselves while living on the street. The life-threatening behaviour in which these young people were engaged evoked these changes in child-care principles. Although these changes were seen by some as further encroachment on the rights of individuals, it was advocated that such intrusive measures had to be undertaken because of the threat to the child and society.

The Toronto Street Youth project was highlighted as an example of a successful child crisis intervention institutional response. The program, with its three phases, provides opportunities for children to stabilize their environments and become empowered to make the necessary healthy changes in their lives. The highly trained and specialized counselling staff and their commitment to treat the children with respect and dignity ensure that many young people choose to leave prostitution.

Law enforcement institutions were also struggling to develop an effective response to these out-of-control kids. The law enforcement response profiled here was certainly an untraditional method. The law enforcement unit detailed within this study was able to move beyond exercising criminal sanctions as the only method of controlling behaviour to embrace a more child-centred approach. This shift in emphases ensured that the social services and police agencies were working together to meet the needs of these children in crisis. Although the police utilized criminal sanctions to control the street pimps, the police embraced social science principles to envision the child as a victim of environmental circumstances.

There is little doubt that the overwhelming success of these programs was due to the sharing of philosophies and approaches to young people in crisis. Subsequently, a cooperative spirit transpired between these agencies because of the sharing of ideology and philosophy. This can be used to demonstrate what can be done when institutional and individual agendas and aspirations are put aside in order to focus on the overall objective of the agencies. The agencies profiled within this exercise demonstrate that institutions can work together and this will, for the most part, ensure success if organizational and individual barriers are lowered to facilitate cooperative, professional, efficient and effective human services.

CHAPTER 10

Emergent Sociological
Theoretical Approaches:
Reviewing the Findings

The pimp's role remains central in the prostitute's life during their association. As disclosed, the pimp hierarchy is structured, organized and operated under the guise of affection or the use of deceit to psychologically coerce and physically compel women to engage in acts of prostitution. Regardless of which method of procurement the pimp employs and the subsequent relationship that develops between the pimp and prostitute, the data clearly illustrate that it is a relationship in which the prostitute will suffer violence at the hands of a pimp.

The pimp-prostitute relationship, informed by sociological approaches, takes on the elements of the sociology of deviance/gender relations. The sociology of gender relations informs the study of deviance, crime and conformity in delineating the contexts of interactions of relationships. An often ignored feature of deviance pertains to such generic processes like dependency.

Emergent sociological theoretical approaches expressed within the social site of prostitution are offered here to provide a theoretical basis and understanding of the many social elements expressed within this site. Sociological theoretical approaches are offered to highlight the underlying social and cultural conditions that give rise to young people perceiving prostitution as a feasible option. The application of sociological theory to this social site allows the reader to further understand some of the correlational responses to social conditions and events. The theoretical approaches to be examined within this chapter include: *cultural deviance, strain, differential association, delinquency and drift, control, labelling* and conclude with the application of *conflict theory.*

Cultural Deviance Theory

The application of cultural deviance theory in this context relies on Walter B. Miller's (1958) version of understanding what motivates young people to become involved in delinquent behaviour. Cultural deviance theories generally view delinquent behaviour as the result of norms, values and beliefs that may be expressed within the young person's cultural context, even though they may be in direct contrast to the dominant or larger cultural norms. Cultural deviance theory suggests that all cultures have individual, distinct norms and values that may be outside the dominant cultural model. When elements such as youth, social isolation and economic deprivation are experienced, young people may develop their own distinct group norms, values and beliefs. Miller argues that "focal concerns" for the lower-class youth may emerge that are substantially different from the wider cultural focal concerns. Again, the cause of these new distinct cultural norms and values is due to the young person's experiences of lower-class isolation and economic deprivation. These distinct focal concerns of the lower class, as argued by Miller, are trouble, toughness, smartness, excitement, fate and autonomy.

Trouble, as illustrated by Miller, suggests that young people within the lower-class culture may see non-law-abiding behaviour as a good thing as it may raise the young person's social status within this culture. The negative stigma attached to getting into trouble by the dominant culture may not be a value within the lower-class culture. Toughness is expressed by physical prowess and is demonstrated by the street image of a tough guy who is fearless, hard and a good fighter. Smartness is the ability to outsmart, outfox, outwit, dupe, con or take others in order to receive material goods and, therefore, raise the young person's social status. Excitement is expressed within this subculture as "going out on the town," a phrase that also indicates that alcohol, drugs or other devices may be used and encouraged. The type of activities engaged in to find the "thrill" within this subculture extends beyond the conventional or normative acceptance. Fate is expressed in the notion that young people in this subculture feel that their lives are subject to forces over which they do not have any control. The resulting behaviour may be directed by the notion that their lives are being guided by lucky or unlucky moments or circumstances. Fate may encourage the lower-class person to gamble with their life or their future by getting involved in very risky behaviour. Autonomy is expressed by the desire for personal independence because young people living in this culture may feel controlled by external forces much of the time. The many controlling

Table Twelve

Focal Concerns of Lower-class Culture

Area	Perceived Alternatives	
1. Trouble	Law-violating behaviour	Law-abiding behaviour
2. Toughness	Physical power, skill, "masculinity," daring, fearlessness, bravery	Weakness, ineptitude, effeminacy, timidity, cowardice, caution
3. Smartness	Ability to outsmart, dupe, "con;" gaining money by "wits," shrewdness, in repartee	Gullibility, slowness, dull-wittedness, gaining money by hard work
4. Excitement	Thrill, risk, danger, change, activity	Boredom, "deadness" safeness, sameness, passivity
5. Fate	Favoured by fortune	Being ill-omened, being unlucky
6. Autonomy	Freedom from external constraint, freedom from superordinate authority, independence	Presence of external constraint, presence of strong authority, dependency, being cared for

elements, such as family, school, police, courts and social workers, may turn these young people further towards their peers in order to distance themselves from the controlling dimensions of these agencies. Table Twelve illustrates Miller's (1958:12) focal concerns of lower class culture.

Applying Miller's lower-class cultural theory directly to adolescent prostitution reveals many sociological explanations for the activities and behaviours within the subculture of prostitution. The data collected for this exercise clearly illustrate that a high level of economic deprivation or uncertainty is experienced by young people when they arrive on the street. The self-reports clearly depict that most of the women arrive on the streets with little economic resource or planning. Regardless of which method the pimp employed to procure these women, the intention was always to generate monetary benefits. Even the young people who came from reasonably secure economic circumstances usually lost all economic opportunity or attachment upon their arrival on the streets. Their relatively hopeless and helpless social circumstances propelled them towards the subcultural norms and values of the street.

The focal concerns of this culture as exposed by Miller can certainly be applied to the social site of prostitution. The notion of trouble or engaging in law-violating behaviour is emphasized within the subculture of prostitution. The data clearly depict that pimps convince the women that participating in acts of prostitution is very much an acceptable behaviour within the street cultural norms. Ostracizing people outside the subculture as "squares" and referring to people participating in prostitution acts as "live" illustrates the challenge to the dominant cultural values of acceptable levels of behaviour. Within this street subculture, the emphasis is on participating in law-violating behaviours such as prostitution, drug use, robbery and theft. These illegal behaviours become "everyday activities" within the prostitution environment.

The element of toughness can also be applied to this social site in highlighting the emphasis of the pimp's physical prowess and social status. The prostitute's ability to withstand the physical and psychological demands of prostitution is also seen as a level of toughness. The women are rewarded and encouraged to work long hours. Their social status is enhanced by the number of tricks they can turn in one day, the amount of money they can demand, and theability to stand their ground when faced with hostile dates, prostitutes or pimps. The prostitute who demonstrates physical prowess, skill, fearlessness, bravery and daring is seen as very street wise and is a sought-after commodity.

Smartness is also a characteristic that is encouraged and developed within this subculture. The ability to get extra money by wits and shrewdness is encouraged. Prostitutes are required to get the most money possible for sex acts and, in some cases, are encouraged to elicit money for sexual acts and leave with the money without engaging in the acts. "Ripping off" dates is often encouraged and can bring much praise. Moreover, the ability to outsmart the cops or morality officers is very much a value. A prostitute who can recognize cops or undercover police operations and evade detection and apprehension is revered within this subculture.

Excitement, fate and autonomy are values that are exercised and enhanced within the prostitution lifestyle. The whole "every night is a Saturday night" concept is a good illustration of the level of excitement demanded and encouraged within this subculture. The high-risk behaviours, the dangers and thrills that this environment engenders are elements that are greatly reinforced.

The fate of young prostitutes is another characteristic that is highlighted in many of the self-reports. The idea that the young woman's fate is in the hands of other elements is often expressed as she believes that her life is being guided and directed by lucky or unlucky circumstances or events. The reliance on "other forces" to depict or control their lives is best illustrated by the woman's engagement in gambling with her life, in high-risk behaviours such as prostitution. The level of autonomy experienced by the prostitutes varied. One element was constant in that the prostitution subculture gave the women some perceived control over their lives outside, and often removed from, the conventional controlling agencies of family, school or state. Many of the prostitutes disclosed a feeling of power or autonomy in their ability to be in charge of negotiating sex acts, location and monetary value for such acts. Although they are very much controlled by their pimps, they are somewhat free from external societal constraints and experience levels of perceived independence while working the streets. Subsequently, a level of perceived autonomy may be experienced by the prostitute, and certainly the pimp discovers autonomy in taking on the authority and independence of managing sex trade workers. Table Thirteen symbolizes the application of Miller's (1958) theory to the prostitution environment.

Strain Theory

The strain theory adopted here will be from the efforts of Merton's (1957) theory of anomie, which suggests that delinquency is a consequence of the frustration that young persons feel when they are unable to achieve the cultural goals they desire through legitimate institutional means. Cultural goals are what people believe are worth striving to obtain. These cultural goals include such items as material possessions, social status and prestige. The institutional means are the socially acceptable methods that define, regulate and control the way that a person obtains these cultural goals. A specific cultural goal may be attained in a variety of means; however, not all of these means are likely to be socially acceptable by the dominant culture.

Merton argues that the cultural goals and institutional means must be reasonable and well balanced if a culture is to be stable and run smoothly. Merton suggests that if a society believes that a particular goal is important, that society should have access to the legitimate institutional means of attaining it. When a society lacks the legitimate institutional means, then a state of normlessness or

Economic Segregation	Distinct Lower-Class Culture	Unique Lower-Class Focal Concerns
Young people arrive on street. Very little opportunities in so-called legitimate economy. Young people brought together because of severe economic conditions on the street. →	Street survival techniques bring young people together: shared values, norms and beliefs at street level. Prostitution environment generates distinct subcultural norms and values. →	Prostitution subcultural norms and values generate unique street focal concerns: trouble, roughness,smartness, excitement, fate and autonomy are all values expressed within this environment

→ = Lower-class delinquency: male or female getting involved in prostitution environment

anomie develops. Merton (1957:198) contends that contemporary American society "approximates the polar type in which great emphasis upon certain success-goals occurs without equivalent emphasis upon institutional means." For example, the lower-classes are presented with images of wealth and material acquisitions and are directed to orientate their behaviour towards accumulating such wealth; however, the legitimate institutional means may be limited or not attainable for them. Subsequently, the individual will most likely utilize methods outside of what is socially acceptable to realize cultural goals.

Merton (1938:676) developed a typology that illustrates the modes of adaptation that are used when a individual is confronted with anomie. Table Fourteen lists these two types of adaptation. The plus sign signifies acceptance and a minus sign denotes rejection. If an individual has the cultural goals and the institutional means, then anomie is absent and the individual will conform to societal norms. However, when the cultural goals are present but the legitimate institutional means are not present, then the individual will become involved in innovation to obtain the goals in illegitimate ways. Unable to "make it" by socially acceptable ways, an individual will pursue the success goal in law-violating ways.

Merton's Theory of Anomie		
Modes of Adaptation	Cultural Goals	Institutional Means
1) Conformity	+	+
2) Innovation	+	-

Source: Robert K. Merton, "Social Structure and Anomie," *American Sociological Review*, 3 (1938), 676.

The application of the prostitution environment to Merton's theory of anomie highlights the innovation category. Both pimps and prostitutes could be viewed as innovators under this model. Pimps do desire the many cultural goals of monetary success and social status, but they are marginalized socially, educationally and economically. Pimps, therefore, do not have the opportunity of utilizing the legitimate institutional means to realize these cultural goals. As innovators, the pimps employ street survival tactics to obtain status and monetary advantage.

The young prostitute can also be seen as fitting within this model as an innovator. She has cultural goals and expectations in regards to family and family life; however, experiences are such that the cultural goals of family are not being experienced. The dysfunctional aspects of her family experience force her to run from the family environment and seek refuge on the street. It can be argued that she is seeking institutional means in response to her family circumstances; however, once she arrives on the street, she is ill-equipped to participate in legitimate institutional means of acquiring material wealth and control and, therefore, will innovate to reach her cultural goals. Some young people will become involved in theft, robbery, drug dealing or prostitution as innovative methods of realizing cultural goals and expectations.

Differential Association Theory

Edwin H. Sutherland's (1947) differential association theory projects that young people learn to commit crimes from others. Sutherland believed that delinquency, like any other form of behaviour, is a product of social interaction. Sutherland contends that individuals are constantly influenced and changed as they interact with small, intimate groups. Our societal expectations and points of view are influenced and developed by our interaction with our intimate peer groups. Sutherland's theory of differential association is outlined here in nine propositions:

1) Criminal behaviour, like other behaviour, is learned from others. That is, delinquent behaviour is not an inherited trait but rather an acquired one.

2) Criminal behaviour is learned through a youth's active involvement with others in a process of communication. The process includes both verbal and nonverbal communication.

3) The principal part of learning criminal behaviour occurs within intimate personal groups. The meanings derived from these intimate relationships are far more influential for adolescents than any other form of communication, such as movies and newspapers.

4) When criminal behaviour is learned, the learning includes techniques of committing the crime, which are sometimes very simple, and the specific direction of motives, drives, rationalizations and attitudes. For example, a youth may learn how to "hot wire" a car from a delinquent companion with which he is involved; he also acquires from others the attitudes or "mind set" that will enable him to set aside the moral bounds of the law.

5) The specific direction of motives and drives is learned from definitions of legal codes as favourable and unfavourable. Adolescents come into contact both with persons who define the legal codes as rules to be observed and with those whose definitions of reality favour the violation of the legal codes. This creates cultural conflict; the next proposition explains how this conflict is resolved.

6) A person becomes delinquent because of an excess of definitions favourable to violation of law over definitions unfavourable to violation of law. This proposition expresses the basic principle of differential association. A person becomes delinquent, then, because he or she has more involvement with delinquent peers, groups or events than with non-delinquent peers, groups or events. Both an excess of contacts with delinquent definitions and isolation from anti-delinquent patterns are important.

7) Differential associations may vary in frequency, duration, priority and intensity. The impact that delinquent peers or groups have upon a young person depends on the frequency of the social contacts, over how long a period of time the contacts take place, the age at which a person experiences these contacts and the intensity of these social interactions.

8) The process of learning criminal behaviour by association with criminal and anti-criminal patterns involves all the mechanisms that are involved in any other learning. The learning of delinquent behaviour is not restricted to mere imitation of other's behaviour.

9) Though criminal behaviour is an expression of general needs and values, it is not explained by those general needs and values because non-criminal behaviour is an expression of the same needs and values. The motives for delinquent behaviour are different from those for conventional behaviour because they are based on an excess of delinquent definition learned from others.

Sutherland (1947) asserts that non-conforming behaviour must be sought or learned from significant others. Table Fifteen symbolizes these assertions.

In applying the social site of prostitution to differential association theory it becomes most evident that learned behaviour is paramount in influencing the prostitution environment. The self-reports clearly demonstrate how pimps articulate and model conflicting definitions about appropriate behaviour. The prostitution environment generates many conflicting definitions about the appropriateness of prostitution-related behaviour. The pimps spend much of

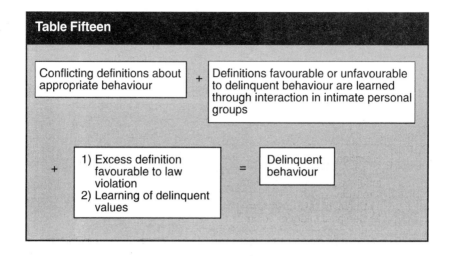

Table Fifteen

Conflicting definitions about appropriate behaviour	+	Definitions favourable or unfavourable to delinquent behaviour are learned through interaction in intimate personal groups

+	1) Excess definition favourable to law violation 2) Learning of delinquent values	=	Delinquent behaviour

their time demonstrating the societal contradictions regarding prostitution and provide favourable reasons for getting involved in prostitution. The application of the differential association model highlights that pimps challenge previously learned norms, values and beliefs in their attempts to have the prostitute learn and adopt new normative values that are acceptable within the subculture. Pimps and prostitutes become the young person's intimate personal group. They provide the opportunity to learn the prostitution techniques, but more importantly they generate new values, norms and expectations within this subculture. The young prostitute not only learns the techniques, but learns, internalizes and accepts the norms and values of the environment. The learning and internalizing of these new values, norms and techniques serves to ensure that the woman bonds to the prostitution environment and begins working as a prostitute.

Drift Theory

David Matza's (1964) drift theory suggests that young people get involved in delinquent activities because juveniles neutralize themselves from the moral bounds of the law and thus "drift" into engaging in delinquent behaviour. Matza (1964:28) notes that drift means that:

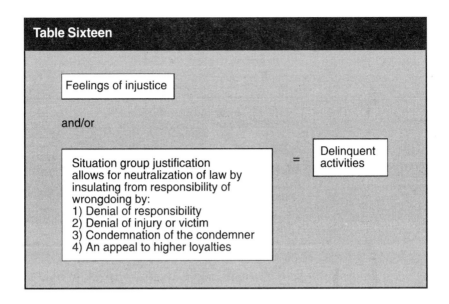

Table Sixteen

Feelings of injustice

and/or

Situation group justification allows for neutralization of law by insulating from responsibility of wrongdoing by:
1) Denial of responsibility
2) Denial of injury or victim
3) Condemnation of the condemner
4) An appeal to higher loyalties

= Delinquent activities

The delinquent transiently exists in limbo between convention and crime, responding in turn to the demands of each, flirting now with one, now the other, but postponing commitment, evading decisions. Thus he drifts between criminal and conventional action.

There are many similarities between differential association and Matza's concept of drift. However, drift theory places much greater importance on the feelings of injustice that juveniles experience, which can be conveyed to situational group justification for activities and behaviours. The situational group justification allows for the neutralization of the law or the insulation of the young person from feeling morally bound to follow the existing social order. The young person can neutralize the law by utilizing four categories as offered by Matza (1957:664-66) in suggesting that the young person claims denial of injury to the victim, denial of responsibility, condemnation of the condemner or an appeal to higher loyalties. Table Sixteen symbolizes the drift process.

Applying the prostitution environment to drift theory reveals that many of the prostitutes and pimps interviewed for this study did experience or perceive feelings of injustice from the dominant culture. Feelings of exclusion, denial, betrayal, hopelessness and helplessness were all manifest in feelings of injustice and resentment for the so-called normative cultural structure. These feelings move the individual into street subcultures where the "situational group justification allows for neutralization of the law" (Matza: 1957:665). As disclosed, the immersion of a young person into the prostitution subculture quickly indoctrinates the individual to the norms, values and beliefs of the street. The pimps, during their training and development of prostitutes, utilize the neutralization techniques by proclaiming the denial of responsibility, denial of injury or victim, condemnation of the condemner and appeal to higher loyalties. The neutralizing techniques serve to internalize the norms and values of the street subculture; therefore, prostitution-related activities will be engaged in without much regard or moral guilt.

Control Theory

Control theorists argue that human beings must be held in check, or controlled in some way, if delinquent activities are to be minimized. Control theorists suggest that delinquency is the result of a deficiency in the socialization of the young person. Juveniles will commit delinquent acts because one of the socially controlling aspects is absent or defective. Travis Hirschi (1969) is the theorist most closely linked with social control or bonding theory and argues that delinquent behaviour is directly related to the quality of the bond that a individual maintains with society. Hirschi (1969:16) notes that "delinquent acts result when an individual's bond to society is weak or broken." Hirschi argues that basic human instincts push young people towards becoming involved in delinquent activities unless there is a social reason for them not to be involved in such behaviour. Hirschi suggests that individuals who are most tightly bonded to social groups such as family, school and peers are less likely to commit delinquent acts. This social bond is made up of four main characteristics: attachment, commitment, involvement and belief.

The first element of the social bond is the individual's "attachment" to conventional others. Hirschi argues that the attachment is expressed in sensitivity towards others and the ability to internalize norms and develop a conscience. The attachment to others also includes the ties of affection and respect that children have for parents, teachers and friends. The assumption here is that the stronger the attachment to others, the more likely it is that an individual will take this into consideration when or if they are tempted to get involved in delinquent activities. Obviously the attachment to parents is the most important variable insulating a child from delinquent activities. Even if the child is coming from a broken home, the child needs to maintain attachment to one or both parents to be fully emotionally nourished. Hirschi (1969:86) claims that "if a child is alienated from the parent, he will not develop an adequate conscience or superego."

The second element of the bond is "commitment" to conventional activities and values. Commitment to conventional activities and values is measured by the degree in which the young person is willing to invest time, energy and themselves into conventional activities such as educational goals. It is asserted that when committed young people consider the social cost of delinquent activities, they will use common sense and believe that the risk of losing the investments already made in conventional behaviour is too great. Hirschi (1969) contends that if juveniles are committed to these conventional values and activities, they develop a "stake in conformity" and will refrain from delinquent behaviour.

The third element, "involvement," also protects an individual from delinquent activities. The assumption made here is that the level of involvement in conventional activities leaves no time for delinquent behaviour. Time and energy are limited, and if the young person is involved in conventional activities, he or she will not have time for non-conventional activities. Hirschi (1969:22) argues:

> The person involved in conventional activities is tied to appointments, deadlines, working hours, plans, and the like, so the opportunity to commit deviant acts rarely arises. To the extent that he is engrossed in conventional activities, he cannot even think about deviant acts, let alone act out his inclinations.

Quite simply, idle minds and time result in boredom and thus the young person will seek out activities that may be outside the conventional norms.

The fourth and last element is "belief;" belief in what the conventional norms and values offer as acceptable ways of behaving. Delinquent behaviour is the result of the absence of effective beliefs that forbid socially unacceptable behaviour. Respect for laws and conventional norms and values is an important component of belief. Respect for values, norms, law and the legal system is engendered and developed from intimate relationships with other conforming people participating in conventional society, especially parents. Hirschi (1969:200) develops a causal chain "from attachment to parents, through concern for the approval of persons in positions of authority, to belief that the rules of

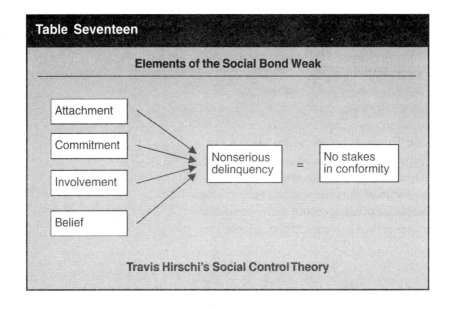

Table Seventeen

Elements of the Social Bond Weak

Attachment

Commitment

Involvement

Belief

Nonserious delinquency

=

No stakes in conformity

Travis Hirschi's Social Control Theory

society are binding on one's conduct." Table Seventeen highlights the elements of the social bond that are necessary to result in "no stakes in conformity."

The application of social control theory to adolescent prostitution reveals many patterns of behaviour that highlight elements of weak social bonds. The self-reports disclose that young women have very limited attachment to conventional others. Many of the women disclosed that attachment is indeed strained, fractured or marginalized from conventional others. The respect that many of the females had for their parents, teachers and friends was greatly reduced as the family environment further eroded. The commitment to conventional activities was subsequently relinquished because of reduced attachment to conventional others. Involvement in conventional activities is limited; therefore, much time is availablefor unconventional activities. The belief in conventional social norms and values was marginalized by adolescent prostitutes, therefore facilitating socially unacceptable behaviour.

Further application of social control theory to the subcultural aspects of street prostitution allows for further understanding of the compelling features of the prostitution environment and lifestyle. Social control theory can expose the elements of the subcultural bond that portray the elements of the subcultural group. This adaptation highlights the attachment, commitment, involvement and belief in the subculture norms and values of the prostitution milieu. This adaptation portrays the elements of the subcultural bond to be strong. The level of attachment to the subcultural group is reinforced in that pimps, prostitutes and street people become the conventional others within this subculture. Again, the data clearly depict very strong attachments to those participants in the prostitution environment. The young prostitute becomes extremely committed to, if not engrossed in, the values and norms embraced within this subculture. The level of involvement in the prostitution subculture results in further isolating the young person with others, like herself, who are playing the game. Obviously, the data demonstrate significant respect for the subcultural norms and values and, therefore, the securing of the attachment, commitment, involvement and belief elements of the subcultural bond. This adaptation of social control theory demonstrates the compelling and conforming nature of the street prostitution subculture.

Labelling Theory

Labelling theory is based on the notion that society creates deviants by labelling those who are perceived as "different" from other individuals. People are only different because they have been "labelled" with a deviant distinction. Labelling theorists focus on the process by which individuals become involved in deviant activities and highlight the role played by social audiences and their responses to the norm violations of individuals. Edwin Lemert (1967) is one of the chief proponents of the labelling perspective in developing the concept of primary and secondary deviance. Lemert purports that primary deviation consists of the behaviour of the individual and secondary deviation is a result of society's response to that behaviour. Lemert suggests that the social reaction to the deviant could be interpreted as forcing a change in status or role. Society's reaction to the deviant individual results in a transformation in the individual's identity; they begin to internalize or play the social role that has been given to them. Individuals begin to see themselves as the label denotes. Social reaction to the deviant individual, whether a disapproving glance or an official level of stigmatization, is crucial to understanding the progression towards a deviant lifestyle. Lemert (1967:94) highlights this process of becoming deviant as having the following stages:

> The sequence of interaction leading to secondary deviation
> is roughly as follows: (1) Primary deviation; (2) Social

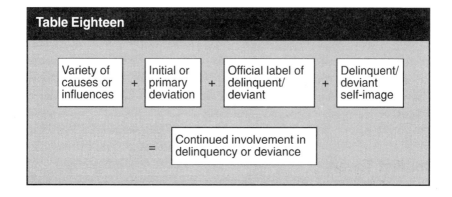

Table Eighteen

Variety of causes or influences	+	Initial or primary deviation	+	Official label of delinquent/deviant	+	Delinquent/deviant self-image

$$= \text{Continued involvement in delinquency or deviance}$$

penalties; (3) Further primary deviation; (4) Stronger penalties and rejection; (5) Further deviation perhaps with hostilities and resentment beginning to focus upon those doing the penalizing; (6) Crisis reached in the tolerance quotient, expressed in formal action by community stigmatizing of the deviant; (7) Strengthening of the deviant conduct as a reaction to the stigmatizing and penalties; (8) Ultimate acceptance of deviant social status and efforts of adjustments on the basis of the associated role.

The second reaction to deviance is expressed in a process of interaction that the individual internalizes and responds to. Subsequently, the deviant is reacting to and acting out the societal expectations of the label. Once the individual internalizes the societal expectations of the label, the individual will continue with a delinquent career. Table Eighteen highlights these elements of labelling theory.

In applying labelling theory to the social site of juvenile prostitution, it is revealed that at several times during the young female's immersion into the prostitution lifestyle she receives many negative labels. The data reveal that many of the women were stigmatized very early in their activities. The women in this study were often labelled as unmanageable or incorrigible by family, social service agencies and teachers before their episodic "running away" behaviour began. Once she was labelled as being involved in prostitution, the stigmatization process was imposed with much greater vigour. The data report that the women were treated much differently by family, friends, social service workers and teachers once it was disclosed that they had been involved in prostitution. Aspects of the secondary deviation process certainly began to evolve as the women internalized the roles and attitudes of the street subculture. The reaction of all the elements of normative society was such that many of the women, in the self-reports, embarked on the process of becoming deviant very quickly after the primary deviation stage. The stigmatization and the subsequent acceptance of this deviant social status ensures that the young woman becomes further immersed into prostitution.

Conflict Theory

The development of the conflict model embraces the concept of "dialectics." The concept can be traced back to the philosophy of ancient Greece. The term "dialectics" refers to the art of conducting a dispute to bring out the truth by disclosing and resolving contradictions in the arguments of opponents. Karl Marx (1906) moved conflict theory to dialectical materialism, as he contended that the conflict was one of competing economic systems in which the weak must ward off exploitation by the strong or powerful in society. The conflict perspective views social control as an outcome of the differential distribution of economic and political power in society. The conflict approach views delinquent behaviour as grounded in alienation and powerlessness. Delinquency will continue to be a problem until the root causes are addressed. Conflict theorists believe that economic and racial discrimination against the lower classes are the root causes.

Conflict theorists believe that the problem of juvenile delinquency must be viewed as part of the bigger problem of alienation and powerlessness amongst Canadian and American youth. Bartollas (1993:218) highlights the problematic features of alienation and powerlessness amongst young people:

> Young people are excluded from full participation in society's political institutions. Young people lack organized lobbies, have limited voting power and hold few positions of authority. Moreover, youths are subjected to controlling forces by the state, and just like any other subordinate group in society, they have their rights, privileges, and identities defined by the powers to be.

Greenburg (1977:196) also identifies a level of adolescent isolation by projecting that "the exclusion of young people from adult work and leisure activities forces adolescents into virtually exclusive association with one another, cutting them off from alternative sources of validation for the self." Greenburg suggests that the long-term consequences of increased levels of age segregation, created by changing patterns of work and education, have increased the vulnerability of youth to the expectations and the evaluations of their peers. Quinney (1979:227) also highlights the necessity of youth employment:

> Our society emphasizes youth and youth culture while at the same time increasingly excluding youth from gainful and meaningful employment. Youth are being relegated to the consumption sector without the economic means for consumption.

Greenburg (1977) argues that attachments to parents are weakened during the transition from childhood to adolescence in capitalist society, while at the same time heightened sensitivity to peers takes place. Conflict emerges between the adolescent and the adult as new norms, values and beliefs appear to develop. The detachment of youth from the family, along with the emergence of advertising directed towards a teenage market, pressures youth to become involved in a "hedonistic consumption-oriented social life" (Greenburg, 1977:198). This detachment from parents and reliance on peers further weakens the adolescent's social-economic position and generates greater levels of alienation and powerlessness.

In applying conflict theory to juvenile prostitution, the elements of alienation and powerlessness become extreme with brazen distinctions. The pimp-prostitute relationship is one of dependency and is subsequently reinforced by wider cultural values. This research clearly indicates the roles of gender, power and money as instrumental elements in extorting dependency. Although this discussion is limited to the pimp-prostitute association as depicted on the street, it supports many parallels between the characteristics of dependency in the relationships of men and women in conventional or "normative society," according to current literature from feminists who have founded their ideologies on Marxist perspective. The pimp-prostitute relationship, like the men-women relationships depicted in conventional society, are subjected to cultural values that demand that the women take inferior or subservient roles. These cultural values, which are structured and organized within the pimp-prostitute association, demand that this exploitive process continue in order to generate its own existence, which is often depicted in relationships between men and women in conventional society.

The data clearly demonstrate the extreme levels of alienation and powerlessness experienced by young women before and after their immersion into prostitution. Miller (1986), after interviewing sixty-four street prostitutes, concluded that prostitution evolves out of profound social and economic problems confronting adolescent women. Miller further contends that street prostitution was not so much a hustle into which one drifted as it was a survival strategy. As reported earlier, the women interviewed for this study reported difficulties with parents, runaway behaviour and contact with social services or the juvenile justice system. Disorganized, dysfunctional families lives, levels of violence and abuse inside and outside the home, and the resulting running away from those chaotic settings often resulted in the young person's arrest and detention as status offender. The feelings of injustice and disillusionment within their own lives generate accelerated levels of alienation and powerlessness. This enhanced level of alienation and powerlessness makes these young people extremely vulnerable to street subcultures and specifically ripe for exploitive encounters with pimps and others endorsing a prostitution agenda.

The sociological theoretical approaches that have been examined and applied to prostitution in this chapter include cultural deviance, strain, differential association, delinquency and drift, control, labelling and conflict theory. These sociological theoretical approaches expressed and applied to the social site of prostitution have been offered here to expose the theoretical bases and the understanding of the many social elements expressed within this social site. These approaches highlight the underlying social and cultural conditions that develop and emerge to move young people to perceive prostitution as a feasible option. The application of sociological theory to this social site has illustrated the correlational responses to social conditions and events. This analysis of the correlated responses to social environments provides for greater understanding of social activity and allows one to "make sense of the non-sense" by exposing the consequences of social condition and events on human activities.

Conclusion: Reviewing the Findings

In conclusion, this exploratory study has utilized qualitative sociological principles and practices to make sense of the social site of adolescent prostitution. This study has facilitated the opportunity to engage applied sociological assessments to understand social phenomena. Sociology provides an opportunity to make sense of our social worlds. Sociological methods of inquiry, informed by sociological theory, stimulate assessments and explanations of social behaviour. Sociology, as a discipline, invites individuals to make sense of the apparent non-sense, to become keen observers of the passing social scene, to challenge our favourite ways of seeing and thinking, to move beyond our gaze, to invoke a critical analysis of our social realities and to make sense of our social environments. Adolescent prostitution is a prominent social phenomena in most urban centres in North America. This exploratory study has invoked sociological assessments to allow for greater sociological understanding of adolescent prostitution and the complexities of this subcultural existence. Moreover, this sociological assessment has facilitated an analysis of a social site that often denies access to outsiders and is very much misunderstood. This exploratory study examined the interaction between male street sex trade managers (pimps) and female street sex trade workers (prostitutes). It asserts that pimps are indeed primary actors in producing and reproducing the subculture of street prostitution. The pimp is very central in the prostitute's life and invokes various strategies to ensure the immersion of women into prostitution.

The qualitative methodology exercised within this text highlights the applied and theoretical features of conducting social research. The methodological process is emphasized in this effort to inform the reader of the many problematic characteristics of capturing social phenomena. From the observation of social phenomena to generating a hypothesis, to isolating the phenomena and exposing the many problematic factors included in research design, this study allows the reader to experience the methodological concerns and debates that influence the collection of data, analysis and, therefore, the results. Since research results are no better than the methods utilized to get them, this study exposes the struggles and complexities of conducting social research. The methodology naturalized in this text characterizes the social action and interaction that encompasses the social organization of prostitution. This methodological design demonstrates the utilization of numerous sources of inquiry such as review of scholarship, research related literature, content analysis of secondary data sources, field observation and intensive interviews in order to present an accurate depiction of the social site of adolescent prostitution.

This qualitative exercise provided the opportunity to develop a social typology of juvenile prostitution that identifies the characteristics of the women who are involved in prostitution. Specifically, reference to such dimensions as social background, family composition and characteristics, history of abuse, levels of formal education, age, socioeconomic status, physical and mental health, race and drug usage are all elements that were assessed to formulate this social typology. The concluding social typology portrays a bleak, if not desperate, image of a vulnerable, exploited and victimized individual who is destined to a troubled existence. These young women are not running to the streets but are running from acute crisis circumstances and experiences in their home environments. These children and adolescents arrive on the street in an extremely physically and psychologically vulnerable condition. The dysfunctional aspects of their family life varied, but, consistently, the issue of the inability to live with family members was present. A significant number come from single parent households and most reported some level of either sexual, physical or psychological abuse in their lives. Most of the respondents did not proceed past the Grade Nine level of formal education and they represented various levels of income groups. The physical and mental health of these adolescents can only be described as extremely desperate, vulnerable, volatile and self-destructive. These adolescents are at various stages of mental and physical crisis when they are immersed into a street environment that shows no mercy.

The methods that pimps use to procure women into prostitution are emphasized to demonstrate the interaction of street pimps and their subcultural roles as played out within this street environment. A pimp who discovers a young woman in a vulnerable condition utilizes the seduction method of procurement. A pimp who discovers a woman in a less vulnerable condition appears to use a stratagem method of procurement. Pimps seduce women into prostitution by strategically displaying various levels of affection, admiration, consideration and concern. These elements of emotional support serve to bond the woman to the pimp and subsequently to prostitution. The psychological and emotional coercion and manipulation that are exercised during this method of procurement are most successful in motivating these vulnerable women.

The stratagem method of procurement highlights that the pimp's approach is very direct in articulating that he wants the woman to work for him as a prostitute. Pimps disgorge an ideology to these women that promises large amounts of money, the glamour of travel and adventure. Pimps exhort that they can assist women in developing this new lucrative, romanticized career and promise to provide all the necessary support and protection.

The training process exposed the job-training strategies and orientation procedures that pimps employ in preparing women for prostitution. Moreover, this examination reveals the sociological process and the subcultural components that are engendered and imposed while learning the prostitution game. The socialization process and the subcultural components exposed the strategies that pimps utilize to indoctrinate new recruits to conform without question to the rules, expectations and roles as imposed by pimps and the street environment. The significance and importance of being "turned out" is that it allows for rigorous adhesion to set rules and regulations, but most consequential is the ensuring of ideological adherence to the prostitution subculture. The ideological adherence not only serves as a technique of neutralization of the stigma attached to the sex trade by the dominant culture but also facilitates the internalization of the prostitution role. The woman's internalization of the prostitution role prescribes her to think, act, walk, talk and live the foreseen social role of a street prostitute. She begins to see herself as labelled, living, acting and thinking as a prostitute.

The relationship that the new prostitute has with her pimp continues to demonstrate the characteristics of a boyfriend-girlfriend or a manager-worker association; however, it is a relationship that quickly begins to degenerate into conflict and subsequent physical violence. The data present a disturbing litany of incidents in which the pimp-prostitute relationship descends to various levels of violence. This violence ensures the prostitute's compliance with the pimp's domain. The obvious consequences of this exploitation are manifest in the many fears, the limited disclosure, physical and mental endangerment and an emerging cycle of violence that forces the woman to remain in the prostitution environment.

Pimps generate employment strategies by monopolizing on violence, exercising imagery and maintaining a hierarchical structure to ensure the social order of the sex trade. Pimps advise prostitutes that they need protection on the street and advocate that they will protect them from all the evils of the street. Analysis of this claim of protection reveals that pimps have set up an enterprise in which they have created a demand for their own services. Pimps do indeed provide protection for street prostitutes, but the protection is established to guard against other pimps who are diligently attempting to acquire the prostitute's revenue generating capabilities. Pimps employ a hierarchy on the street to determine and enhance their image as keen, tough and prudent entrepreneurs. The many factors that ascertain where a pimp is positioned within this hierarchy include the number of players involved, possession of material items and the ability to secure respect on the street.

Many social services and law enforcement institutions have adopted programs and methods to police the street sex trade. A significant number of social services institutions have moved to a mandated child welfare model. Many law enforcement institutions have moved to a child-centred approach. This change in policy entails that social service and law enforcement agencies work together to ensure that the needs of children in crisis were being met. The overwhelming success of these programs is due to the sharing of philosophies and approaches to young people in crisis.

The data reveal a very disturbing portrayal of victimization, abuse, violence, exploitation and social decay that is experienced by many young people in Canada and the United States. Much needs to be done to address this serious social problem. Children and adolescents continue to participate in self-destructive behaviours in the 1990s and the forecasts suggest escalating numbers of young people will continue to involve themselves in high-risk activities. This forecast of more human degradation clearly calls for more innovative programs and designs that will not just react to this social blight but will prevent children from having to make detrimental life choices.

Prevention of social problems requires a complete analysis and understanding of the root causes of the participant's behaviour and the emerging social phenomena. This text has demonstrated the link between factors such as family, community, school, peers and the state as contributing to the young person's social demise. Preventive policies need to address the diminutive responses and conditions of the social institutions in the young person's life. This text has revealed the disconcerting numbers of children and families living below the poverty line and the implications bestowed on children due to social and economic restrictions. Social decay virtually begins at birth for many of these children. Equality of condition and equality of opportunity are never experienced or afforded to these families who are experiencing various levels of economic and social crisis. Within the school system the children are further marginalized to limited participation in the dominant culture. Social policy needs to provide for empowerment strategies to engage families and, subsequently, the young people to fully participate in society to prevent further socially destructive behaviours.

The preventive social policy advocated within this exploratory study projects a social justice model. This social justice model embraces proactive and preventive strategies that address the many social injustices in our communities. The social justice model, its emphases being within the philosophy of the welfare state, promotes the cooperation of people in providing a united socially enriched community so that every member has an equal and real opportunity to grow and live to the best of their abilities. These ideal conditions of social justice through social union are essentially those of democracy. The emphases here challenge our current social and political policies of "reactionary responses" to juvenile prostitution or other socially destructive behaviours.

The social justice model asks for the development of programs and policies to enrich and empower the lives of citizens in order to prevent socially destructive behaviour from occurring. The assumption here is that when young people realize equality of opportunity and condition, they will not become involved in delinquent behaviour.

The right to social justice in our communities could be summarized to illustrate sound social and political policies that allow every child a normal healthy birth, a healthy home and social environment, abundant good food, appropriate education, and effective intervention programs and strategies to identify children at risk and effectively respond to their needs. The social justice model argues for every mature person a secure job adapted for his or her abilities and for all persons an income adequate to maintain them efficiently in the position of their highest social service. All persons should be afforded such influences with authorities that their needs and ideas receive due consideration. The social justice model provides social and economic opportunities for the citizenry, which would result in the decreasing necessity and incidence of people involved in crime or delinquent activities, the decrease of people being victimized by crime or social decay and a reduction of the reactionary crime control apparatus.

The characteristics of the social justice model and its emphasis on the welfare of the individual and the community provide an alternative approach to individuals involved in delinquent activities. The criminal justice model within the social justice mandate focuses on providing the offender with many opportunities to relinquish deviant activities. The general features project informality, generic referrals, individualized sentencing and indeterminate sentencing. The key personnel to operationalize this model are child-care experts and social workers. The key agencies would, therefore, be the social work and social service agencies that are assigned the task of diagnosis of individual problems and analysis of the individual's social environments. The understanding of client behaviour is environmentally determined under this model and the purpose of intervention is to provide treatment or *parens patriae* in the case of juveniles. The overall objective of this model is to respond to individual needs in order to facilitate rehabilitation (Corrado et al.,1992).

This conceptual analysis of the pimp-prostitute relationship argues for an alternative social response that adequately appraises the exploitive, degrading aspects of this association between male sex trade managers and female sex trade workers. Pimps subject prostitutes to a lifestyle that stimulates various levels of exploitation, violence, degradation, dominance and manipulation, regardless of which game the pimp chooses to play. The pimp is a "master of a game," a destructive game that women cannot win.

Glossary of Terminology Used within the Pimp-Prostitute Subculture

Bad date – A customer that imposes or has imposed some sort of threat to the prostitute, e.g., assaults, thefts.

B.J. – Oral sex performed on a male by the prostitute.

Boyfriend – Used often in reference to a pimp.

Broke – To complete the act of sex for money—brake

Choose – The process of the female deciding if she is going to work as a prostitute and/or which pimp she is going to work for, often called "Choosing time."

Chump-off – When the prostitute takes off from the pimp, also means the prostitute was goofing off.

Colour of right – Claim of rightful, lawful ownership or title over property.

Dates – Customers of prostitutes.

Family – Term used by pimps and prostitutes to describe their immediate friends and other prostitutes.

Flying the guy – Playing a role of listening to rap music, break dancing and partying. Status judged by the number of girls that can be "picked up" and the level of participation in shoplifting to display an extravagent lifestyle.

Half and half – Performing oral sex on customer followed bysexual intercourse.

Hand job – Masturbation performed on customer by prostitute.

Ho[e] – Prostitute.

Jacked up – Means robbed; usually expressed when the prostitute has had her money taken from her by a pimp, bad date or another prostitute.

John – Customer of prostitute.

Kicking – Working as a pimp.

Lady – Prostitute.

Lay – Sexual intercourse.

Life on the track – Living day to day within the prostitution environment.

Live – Working as a prostitute or knowing about the prostitution game.

Mack or mac – Top pimp, pimp in charge.

Main lady – Usually the prostitute that the pimp trusts the most, wife-in-law.

Man – Pimp.

Player – Apprentice pimp or helper.

Qualified – Being fully trained and eligible to work as a prostitute.

Safe – Condom.

Square – One who does not work as a prostitute.

Street charge – Fee demanded by pimps for training and preparing a recruit to become a prostitute; usually invoked against prostitute if she wishes to leave the pimp or work for another pimp—leaving fee.

Stroll – The area of streets where the street prostitutes work and the "prostitution game" is played.

Track – The area where prostitutes apply their trade.

Trap – Money earned by completing acts of prostitution.

Turning Out – Preparing and training a woman to become a prostitute.

Trick – Customer of prostitute.

Wife-in-law – The pimp's main or trusted prostitute.

Bibliography

Allain, Jane and Marilyn Pilon. "Prostitution." *Current Issue Review: Library of Parliament.* Revised May 31, 1993.

Badgley Report. *Sexual Offenses Against Children in Canada.* Ottawa: Canadian Government Publishing Centre, 1984.

Bagley, Chistopher, Barbara Burrows and Carol Yaworski. "Street Kids and Adolescent Prostitution: A Challenge For Legal And Social Services." In *Canadian Child Welfare Law: Canadian Families and the State.* Toronto: Thompson, 1991.

Bagley, Christopher and Loretta Young. "Juvenile Prostitution And Child Sexual Abuse: A Controlled Study." *Canadian Journal Of Community Mental Health*, Volume 6, no.1 Spring, 1987, p. 3.

Barry, Kathleen. *Female Sexual Slavery.* New York: New York Press, 1979.

Bart, Pauline and Linda Frankel. *The Student's Sociologists Handbook,* 4th ed. New York: Random House, 1986.

Bartollas, Clemens. *Juvenile Delinquency*, 3rd. ed. New York: Macmillan, 1993.

Becker, Harold K. and B. Geer. "Participant Observation and Interviewing: A Comparison." In W. Filstead, ed. *Qualitative Methodology*. Chicago: Rand McNally, 1970.

Benjamin, Michael. *Juvenile Prostitution: A Portrait Of "The Life."* Toronto: Prepared For The Ministry Of Community And Social Services, n.p., 1995.

Berger, Stan. *Sentencing Those that Exploit Prostitutes*.Toronto: n.p., 1987.

Brannigan, Augustine and John Fleischman. "Juvenile Prostitution And Mental Health: Policing Delinquency of Treating Pathology?" *Canadian Journal of Law and Society*, Volume 4, 1989.

Brantingham, Pat and Patrician Brantingham. *Patterns in Crime*. New York: Macmillan, 1984.

Bureau of Municipal Research. Civic Affairs. *Street Prostitution in our Cities*. Toronto: n.p., 1983,

Canadian Council on Social Development. *Not Enough: The Meaning and Measurement of Poverty in Canada*. Report of the CCSD National Task Force on the Definition and Measurement of Poverty in Canada. Ottawa, 1984.

Caplan, Gerald. "The Facts of Life about Teenage Prostitution." *Crime and Delinquency*, January, 1984.

Corrado, Raymond, et al. *Juvenile Justice in Canada: A Theoretical and Analytical Assessment*. Toronto: Butterworths, 1992.

Davidson, John. *The Stroll*. Toronto: New Canada, 1986.

Doherty Social Planning Consultants. *A Study of the Services Required by Youths Admitted into Casatta-Warrendale*. Toronto: n.p. 1986.

Enables, G. *Juvenile Prostitution in Minnesota: The Report of a Research Project*. St. Pauls: The Enablers, 1978.

Fleischman, John. *Working Papers on Prostitution*. Ontario: Ontario Publishers, 1984.

Fox, Vernon. *Introduction to Criminology*. New Jersey: Prentice Hall, 1976.

Fraser Report. *Pornography and Prostitution in Canada*. Canada: Communications and Public Affairs, 1985.

Garfinkle, Harold. *Studies in Ethnomethodology*. New Jersey: Prentice Hall, 1967.

Goffman, Erving. *Asylums*. New York: Doubleday, 1961.

Greenburg, David. "Delinquency and the Age Structure of Society." *Contemporary Crisis*, 1 (1977).

Greenspan, Edward. *Annotated Criminal Code of Canada*. Toronto: Carswell, 1994.

Harlow, Spark, et al. *Male and Female Adolescent Prostitution: Huckleberry House Sexual Minority Youth Service Project*. Washington, D.C.: U.S. Department of Health and Human Services, Youth Department Bureau, 1981.

Hersch, Patricia. "Coming Of Age On City Streets." In *Psychology Today*. New York, January 1988, p. 23.

Hindman, Jan. *Just Before Dawn: From the Shadows of Tradition to New Relections in Trauma Assessment and Treatment of Sexual Victimiation.* Ontario: Alexandria, 1989.

Hirschi, Travis. *Causes of Delinquency.* Berkeley: University of California Press, 1969.

Hospital for Sick Children. *Sexually Transmitted Infections in Adolescent Prostitutes in Toronto.* Toronto: N.P., 1989.

James, Jennifer. *Entrance into Juvenile Prostitution.* Washington, D.C.: National Institute of Mental Health, 1980.

James, Jennifer and Nanette Davis. "Contingencies in Female Sexual Role Deviance: The Cast of Prostitution." *Human Organization* (Winter, 1982), p. 58.

Kochendorfer, Diane. *Status Report: Casatta/Warrendale - Phase II - Toronto Street Youth Project.* Toronto: N.P. 1986.

Lasswell, Thomas and Jerry Bode. *Sociology in Context: Scientific and Humanistic.* New Jersey: General Learning Press, 1974.

Lemert, Edwin. "The Juvenile Court-Quest and Realities." In *Juvenile Delinquency and Youth Crime*, President's Task Force. Washington, D.C.: Government Printing Office, 1967, p. 37.

Lofland, John and Lyn Lofland. *Analyzing Social Settings: A Guide to Qualitative Observations and Analysis.* California: Wadsworth Publishing, 1984.

Lowman, J. "Taking Young Prostitutes Seriously." *Canadian Review of Sociology and Anthropology*, February, 1987, p. 17.

MacDonnall, Tom. *Never Let Go.* Toronto: Macmillan, 1986.

Maiuro, Roland D., Eric Trupin and Jennifer James. *Sex-Role Differentiation in a Female Juvenile Delinquent Population: Prostitute vs. Control Samples.* American Orthopsychiatric Association, 1983.

Marx, Karl. *Capital: A Critique Of Political Economy.* New York: Random House, 1906.

Mathews, Frederick. "Intervening in Adolescent Prostitution." *Symposium on Street Youth.* Toronto: Convenant House, 1986.

Matza, David. *Delinquency And Drift.* New York: Wiley, 1964.

McCullough, Patricia. *Youth Prostitution.* Lexington, MA: Lexington Books, 1990.

Merton, Robert K. "Social Stucture and Anomie." *American Sociological Review* 3 (1938).

Merton, Robert K. *Social Theory and Social Structure*, 2nd ed. New York: Free Press, 1957.

Miller, Eleanor. *Street Women*. Philadelphia: Temple University Press, 1986.

Miller, Walter. "Lower-Class Culture as a Generation Milieu of Gang Delinquency," *Journal Of Social Issues* 14 (1958), p. 73.

Milner, David. *Black Players*. New York: New York Press, 1973.

Mitchell, Sharon and Laura Smith. *Juveniles in Prostitution: Fact vs. Fiction*. California: R + E, 1984.

Nett, Emily. *Canadian Families: Past and Present*. Toronto: Butterworths, 1988.

Prus, Robert and Styllianoss Trini. *Hookers, Rounders and Desk Clerks*. Toronto: Gage, 1980.

Quinney, Richard. *Criminology*, 2nd ed. Boston: Little Brown, 1979.

Regina vs. Green and Lattermore. *Ontario Provincial Court Proceedings*. Toronto: n.p., 1987.

Regina vs. Morgan. *Ontario District Court Proceedings*. Toronto: n.p., 1986.

Rolland, Maiuro. "Sex-Role Differentiation in a Female Juvenile Delinquent Population." *Orthopsychiat* (April 1983), p. 16.

Rubington, Earl and Martin Weinberg. "Prostitutes." In *Deviance: The Interactionist Perspective*. New York: Macmillan, 1981, p. 73.

Schonborn, K., *Dealing with Violence*. Illinois: Thomas, 1976.

Seng, Magnus. "Child Sexual Abuse and Adolescent Prostitution: A Comparative Analysis." *Adolescence*, Volume 24, no.95 Fall, 1989.

Shultz, David. *Pimp*. New York: New York Press, 1978.

Silbert, Mimi and Ayala Pines. "Early Sexual Exploitation as an Influence in Prostitution." Washington, D.C.: National Association of Social Workers, 1983.

Silbert, Mimi. *Sexual Assault of Prostitutes: Phase One*. Washington, D.C.: National Institute of Mental Health, National Center for the Prevention and Control of Rape, 1980.

Sinclair, Deborah. *Understanding Wife Assault: A Training Manual for Counsellors and Advocates*. Toronto: Ontario Government Bookstore, 1985.

Statistical Abstract of the United States, United States Census Bureau, Washington, D.C., 1993.

Sullivan, Terry. *Juvenile Prostitution: Moral Disturbance of Job Creation Strategy?* Toronto: University of Toronto Press, 1984.

Sutherland, Edwin. *Principles of Criminology.* Philadelphia: Lippincott. 1947.

Sutherland, Edwin. "A Statement Of The Theory." In Albert Cohen et al., ed. *The Sutherland Papers.* Bloomington: Indiana University Press, 1956.

Sykes, Gresham and David Matza. "Techniques Of Neutralization: A Theory of Delinquency." *American Sociological Review* 22 (December 1957).

Toronto Street Youth Project. Toronto: Ministry of Community and Social Services: n.p., 1986.

Visano, Livy. *This Idle Trade.* Concord: VitaSana Books, 1987.

Webber, Marlene. *Street Kids: The Tragedy of Canada's Runaways.* Toronto: University of Toronto Press, 1991.

Weisberg, Kelly. *Children of the Night: A Study of Adolescent Prostitution.* Massachusetts: D.C. Heath and Co., 1985.

Yaworski, Carol. *Mandated Child Care Services.* Toronto, n.p., 1986.